Waterways
past and present

ADLARD
COLES
NAUTICAL

Waterways

past and present

A unique portrait of Britain's waterways heritage

Derek Pratt

Right: The bridge at Dukinfield Junction at Ashton-under-Lyne in eastern Manchester. Looking at canals is an absorbing activity as the photographs in this book prove.

Published by Adlard Coles Nautical
an imprint of A & C Black Publishers Ltd
38 Soho Square, London W1D 3HB
www.adlardcoles.com

First edition published 2006

ISBN 0-7136-7634-5

Printed and bound in Singapore by Star Standard

© Book concept and design 2006
by Fred Barter at Bosun Publications
The Ferry Point, Ferry Lane
Shepperton on Thames
TW17 9LQ

Contents

Times of Change

The second half of the 18th century was a time of change throughout the world. In France and America this manifested itself in bloody revolutions, but in Britain a more peaceful change took place. It became known as the Industrial Revolution, and it was the canals that made it all possible. Led by engineers like James Brindley and financed by businessmen like Josiah Wedgwood, they connected the main rivers and ports with artificial waterways.

A second wave of canal building came during the first quarter of the 19th century. Thomas Telford and his contemporaries had learned the lessons of James Brindley and the pioneer canal builders which were to keep the new canals in a straight line and avoid the earlier meandering, contour hugging waterways. The new canals had deep cuttings and embankments keeping locks bunched together in long flights. Journeys on the older canals were too slow when economic pressure demanded a fast delivery of cargoes.

The Stockton and Darlington Railway opened in 1825 heralding a warning to all inland waterborne transport. Railways were built throughout the country with the same enthusiasm and speculation that had greeted the height of canal building fifty years earlier. The railways didn't have summertime water problems and could still operate in freezing conditions. They could also handle bulk cargoes and were quicker.

During this period the boating families were forced to leave their canalside cottages and move into the cramped boat cabins. The new aggressive competitor meant that costs had to be cut and the boatman could no longer afford to live ashore. An indigenous floating population developed, with their own traditions, that lasted over a hundred years. That period of time saw the slow decline of commercial carrying on most of the canals, with some of them gradually becoming uneconomic and forced to close.

This situation was often accelerated by the purchase of canals by railway companies who then allowed their watery competitor to decline through lack of maintenance.

The boating families who toiled up and down the English canals in 1850 would have still recognised most of the familiar places if a time machine could have propelled them into the mid-20th century. The fabric of the waterways remained constant with its mills and warehouses, wharves and factories. The bridges, locks, tunnels and aqueducts were still there although motor boats had replaced traditional horse-power.

By 1960, the first motorways had made their appearance and the railways began to suffer the kind of competition they had inflicted on the canals over a hundred years earlier. The severe winter of 1962-1963 finally brought an end to regular commercial carrying on the narrow canals.

Project the boatman from 1850 to the start of the 21st century and he would be bewildered to see the changes in his former working environment. The Victorian warehouses and mills have either been demolished or transformed into offices and apartments. New bridges cross the waterways with the cacophony of modern motor transport, and pleasure boats fill the locks and line the banks. Place him at Old Turn Junction or Gas Street Basin in the centre of Birmingham, and he would struggle to find anything recognisable. The same would apply at Paddington Basin or the former Brentford Dock in London. Regent's Canal Dock is now Limehouse Basin, filled with pleasure boats and housing for City workers. Today there are Brindley Houses, James Brindley pubs, Telford Way, Narrowboat Way and Boathorse Hill. All these names refer to new roads, housing developments and commercial science parks, recalling the men who built the canals and worked upon them all those years ago.

7

The Age of Brindley

Was James Brindley the greatest canal engineer? Waterway historians and writers point to the achievements of such worthies as William Jessop, John Rennie and Thomas Telford. All were great men in their time, but Brindley was the pioneer canal engineer whose example was set for all his successors to learn from. When Brindley built Harecastle Tunnel it was the first time anyone had attempted such a monumental feat of engineering. He encountered numerous geological obstacles that took years to overcome but in the end he succeeded. When Telford built his adjacent tunnel fifty years later, most of the problems had been solved and he also had the advantage of more modern surveying methods and civil engineering techniques.

Right: The Packet House at Worsley.
A passenger service began from here to Manchester in 1766, bringing in additional revenue for the Duke of Bridgewater. The entrance to the Duke's mines can be found beyond the bridge in the background.

Above: Statue of James Brindley in the restored canal basin at Coventry. Brindley is remembered by this street name in Birmingham.

The Bridgewater Canal

The canal age began in 1765 with the completion of the Duke of Bridgewater's Canal which connected the Duke's coal mines at Worsley to the centre of Manchester. The contoured canal was lock-free but the engineers, John Gilbert and James Brindley, faced the problem of crossing the River Irwell.

They solved this by constructing a stone aqueduct at Barton which was 200 yards long and 38 feet above the river. This was a considerable achievement at that time and attracted huge crowds to witness its opening in 1761. The aqueduct stayed in use until 1893 when it was replaced by the present Barton Swing Aqueduct over the Manchester Ship Canal.

Left: The entrance to the Duke's mines at Worsley. Inside the mines were about 46 miles of subterranean canal connected by inclined planes. Women and children were employed inside the mines in conditions that were described as horrific. Only the entrance can be seen today, with the water stained orange because of seepage from inside the mine.

Statue of Josiah Wedgwood (1730 – 1795) outside the Wedgwood Visitor Centre at Barlaston near Stoke-on-Trent. He was the chief sponsor for Brindley's Trent and Mersey Canal and built his first ceramics factory by the canal at Etruria.

The Trent and Mersey Canal

Burton-upon-Trent has become universally famous for its production of beer, and many of Britain's main breweries are still located in the town. Like the pottery industry around Stoke, Burton's brewing industry owes much of its success to the Trent and Mersey Canal. Horninglow Wharf was the dividing point where the canal changed from being a wide beamed waterway to a narrow one. The wide canal enabled barges to reach Burton and carry the produce of the brewing industry to Hull for export to Europe and beyond.

Right: The black and white photo shows a very run down **Horninglow Wharf** in April 1976 with a wide-beamed hotel boat in the foreground being painted for the coming season. In the background, the overhanging salt warehouse and its attendant buildings have all been demolished, as is evident by the colour photo taken in 2005 (both photos taken from the same position).

The Trent and Mersey Canal was the first important long distance artificial waterway in Britain. Originally called the Grand Trunk Canal, it made the first inland waterway connection between the North Sea and the Irish Sea. It runs from Shardlow on the River Trent to Preston Brook by the River Mersey where it connects to the Duke of Bridgewater's Canal. Completed in 1777 after eleven years work, it has wide barge size locks at each end but narrow locks in the centre. This set the seven-foot standard gauge for most of Brindley's network of canals. The Trent and Mersey was the start of Brindley's vision of a Grand Cross of canals that eventually would connect the ports of the Humber, Mersey, Severn and Thames with the emerging industrial heartland of the Midlands.

Below: At the eastern end of the Trent and Mersey Canal is Brindley's inland port at Shardlow. Although no longer an active port, it is now a busy boating centre with boatyards and marinas. Many of the original buildings have survived and have been converted to new uses. The building in the background of the photograph is the Clock Warehouse which once handled goods underneath a loading arch. It is now a popular pub and restaurant.

The banks of the Trent and Mersey Canal through Stoke-on-Trent were lined with the distinctive bottle kilns used in the pottery industry. There were over 2000 of these kilns throughout the Potteries, creating fine porcelain and ceramics. Working within these ovens was an arduous task, especially for the boys known as 'sagger maker's bottom-knockers' who worked long hours at the base of the hot kilns. A sagger was a round fireclay box that held ware during firing in the bottle oven and the bottom knocker was an assistant to the saggar maker. Most of the canalside bottle kilns have gone, leaving these two examples at Hanley that stand forlorn amid the ruins of the factory they once served night and day.

Above: The author Arnold Bennett (1867–1931) was born in Hanley and would probably have recognised this row of canal workers', houses. Bennett was a descendant of James Brindley, following the great engineer's affair with Mary Bennett five years before his marriage to Anne Henshall in 1765. Brindley's illegitimate son John was the great-grand-father of the Five Town's novelist. Photographed on a bleak winter's day in January 1973, this row of canal side houses has since been demolished and replaced by modern housing.

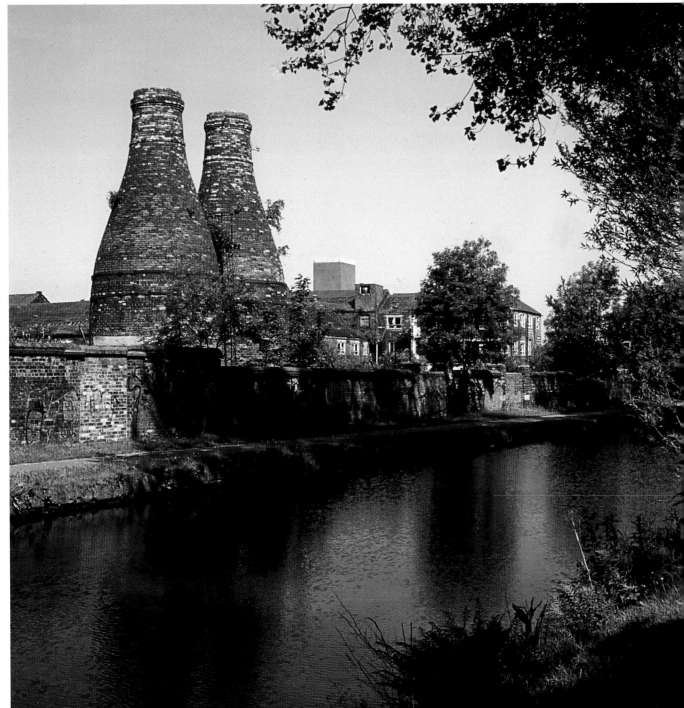

It took eleven years to complete Harecastle Tunnel, by which time Brindley had died through diabetes and overwork. Once open, the canal was extremely busy and the narrow tunnel, soon became a bottleneck. Thomas Telford's adjacent tunnel built in 1827, allowed traffic to run in both directions until Brindley's tunnel finally collapsed through subsidence. Telford's 3,000 yard tunnel is still used today under strict control by tunnel-keepers at each end. The entrance to Brindley's tunnel, can be seen to the right of the one used now. The orange staining in the water is caused by iron ore seepage from mines within Brindley's tunnel.

Left: Originally a slaughterhouse, the Star Inn at Stone became a pub in 1568, predating the canal by two hundred years. In 1940 the citizens of Stone clubbed together and raised £5,000 to build a Spitfire. The plane was named Star of Stone after the pub.

Below: The old brewery at Stone seen on a frosty winter morning. Joule's Brewery was built in Stone in 1758, 13 years before Brindley's Trent and Mersey Canal arrived in the town. The 'Stone Ale' brewed here was exported throughout the world. Alfred Barnard wrote in 1889 'Who has not heard of Stone Ale, that ancient and wholesome beverage, whose praises have been lauded in prose and song for almost 150 years'.

Today, Stone announces itself as 'The Canal Town' where there are locks and several boatyards close to the town centre.

Caldon Canal

The Caldon Canal was built to bring limestone from the hills around Caulden Low to use in the pottery industry at Stoke-on-Trent. It is a branch of the Trent and Mersey with a junction at Etruria near to the original Wedgwood factory. In its early stages the canal is intensely built-up, but once clear of the Potteries urban sprawl it become one of the most picturesque and remote canals on the inland waterway system. The canal splits at Hazelhurst, with one branch going to Leek and the other to Froghall, where it once connected to the now derelict Uttoxeter Canal. It was during the surveying for the Caldon Canal that Brindley caught a cold and became seriously ill, leading to his death in 1772.

Below: The Leek Branch of the Caldon Canal at Hazelhurst. This is moorland scenery at its finest and just a few miles from Stoke-on-Trent. The boat in the picture has just crossed an unusual aqueduct, where one branch of the canal crosses over the other.

Cheddleton Flint Mill by the Caldon Canal was where flint was ground for use in the pottery and ceramic industry. Powdered flint used to whiten pottery was carried by canal to the factories. The ground, calcinated flints were an important part of Josiah Wedgwood's new product called 'creamware'. Calcinated flint, being white, made it an excellent ingredient in the light-coloured pottery that had become popular at the time. The calcination kilns, where flints were heated to make them brittle, can be seen next to the towpath. Two undershot water wheels that drove the grinding machinery still operate on open days. Today, the mills and waterwheels are run by volunteers and are open to the public at weekends.

Above: Restoration of Cheddleton Lock.
The Caldon Canal was closed to navigation in 1961 and could have been lost forever. Its eventual restoration in 1974 was mostly due to the endeavours of volunteers from the Caldon Canal Society and funding from local councils. The picture shows work in progress restoring Cheddleton Lock in September 1973.

Jesse Shirley's Etruscan Bone and Flint Mill at Etruria Junction where the Caldon Canal meets the Trent and Mersey. It was built in 1857 to grind bone and flint for the pottery industry. Now the Etruria Industrial Museum, it retains most of its original machinery and has one of the oldest working steam engines in the country. Since this photograph was taken in 1995, a modern extension to the museum has been erected behind the mill on the bank of the Caldon Canal opposite a statue to James Brindley.

Consall Forge by the Caldon Canal in the Churnet Valley is difficult to find by road. Walk the towpath from Froghall or travel by boat and you find a remote pub, a steam railway and superb scenery. Only the limekilns remain as reminders of Consall Forge's industrial past when it was the centre of the red ironstone industry. In its commercial heyday, boats loaded with ironstone and limestone from the hills beyond Froghall would have streamed past Consall Forge in great numbers. The Cherry Eye Mines closed in 1923, leaving a legacy in the name 'Cherry Eye Bridge' (see photo below left). The bridge has an unusual Gothic arch and can be seen between Consall Forge and Froghall.

Staffs and Worcester Canal

The Staffs and Worcester Canal connects the Trent and Mersey Canal at Great Haywood near Stafford to the River Severn at Stourport. The canal passes through the centre of Kidderminster, but apart from that manages to avoid built-up areas. It is a delightfully rural canal for much of its 46 mile length, despite never being very far from the Black Country. At Stourport, Brindley created a magnificent inland port with a series of basins now used as moorings for a miscellany of river and canal craft.

Below: The sinuous lines of Great Haywood Junction Bridge which marks the junction of Brindley's Trent and Mersey and Staffs and Worcester Canals. Great Haywood has a beautiful setting at the edge of Cannock Chase and is close to Shugborough Hall. Tixall Wide, a nearby ornamental lake that incorporates the canal, was created to appease the local Lord of the Manor.

Bratch Locks on the Staffs and Worcester Canal can be confusing to inexperienced boaters. To all outward appearances they look like interconnected staircase locks, when in fact they are actually separated by a short pound. The three locks are topped by an elegant octagonal toll-house where a full time lock-keeper helps boaters solve the mysteries of negotiating the locks. For years the toll-house, and its surroundings were white-washed as seen in the black and white photo taken in 1975. Since then the entire area has been restored to its original brick and the lockside has been improved – see below taken in 2001.

Right: St Mary's parish church overlooks the Staffs and Worcester Canal at Kidderminster. Carpet factories used to flank the canal, but sadly most of them have been converted to new uses or demolished in favour of supermarkets. Kidderminster has been a carpet centre since 1735 and had a boom period as recent as the 1950s to 1960s. Unfortunately the carpet industry in the town has gone into sharp decline over the last few years. High sandstone cliffs edge the canal in a beautiful wooded section just south of the town centre.

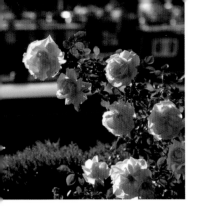

Brindley's inland port at Stourport is at the southern end of the Staffs and Worcester Canal. There was nothing at Stourport before Brindley arrived with his canal in 1766. By 1783 there were brass and iron foundries, a vinegar brewery, spinning mills, carpet factories, boat builders, warehouses, shops and inns. Several canal basins were constructed at different levels connected by locks. The Clock Warehouse, topped by a clock made in 1813, overlooks the Upper Basin. Here too is the 100 room Tontine Hotel built at the time of the canal for visiting merchants. With its position by the River Severn, Stourport has become an inland resort with a variety of pubs and restaurants and even has a permanent fun fair.

Left: Display of roses in a landscaped area next to the Upper Basin at Stourport.

The Coventry Canal

The Coventry Canal has a chequered history. It was originally conceived to connect the Trent and Mersey Canal at Fradley to the Oxford Canal and then on to the River Thames. In doing so it would pass through the rich Warwickshire coalfield, providing Coventry with cheap coal. That section between Coventry and the coalfield was completed by 1769, but by 1771 the money had run out and the canal was still a long way from its northern objective. In the ensuing wrangles James Brindley was sacked. Finally the missing link was built as a joint venture by the Trent and Mersey Canal Company and the Birmingham and Fazeley Canal Company whose canal had recently reached Fazeley.

The Coventry Canal Company later bought this section back but even today some maps still refer to the section between Fazeley and Whittington as the Birmingham and Fazeley Canal.

Below: Hawkesbury, on the northern outskirts of Coventry, is the junction of the Oxford and Coventry Canals. Known as Sutton Stop the junction has long been a meeting place for working boats. It is close to the collieries and had facilities for boating families and a boatman's pub. For some years the Coventry and Oxford Canals ran side by side and remained unconnected because of disputes between the two canal companies.

Below: Joe and Rose Skinner aboard their narrowboat *Friendship* at Sutton Stop, Hawkesbury Junction in February 1974. Joe was the last of the 'Number One' owner boaters working on the Midland canals and one of the last working boatmen to work with a horse in preference to a motor boat. They were retired when this photo was taken, and although they had a cottage nearby they chose to spend most of the day on their boat. *Friendship* has been restored and is now exhibited at the Ellesmere Port Boat Museum.

Above: Working boats moored on the Coventry Canal near Hawkesbury Junction towards the end of the 1960s. These were the remnants of the coal carrying fleets of narrowboats that worked from the local collieries. By now most of the boating families were struggling to make a living.

Below: A pair of working boats on the Coventry Canal in 1958. The lady steering the unpowered butty boat is being towed by her husband on the motor boat. These loaded coal boats were probably en route to a factory in the south.

FRIEND

Cash's Top Shops on the Coventry Canal are about half a mile from the terminal basin. Weavers lived in houses below the factory on the top floor which was a continuous workshop with steam driven looms running the whole length of the row. The workers only had to climb upstairs to start their day's work. The Top Shops, which were built in 1857, produced name-tapes that identified school clothes for children and work clothing for adults.

Above: Information boards have been produced for the large Asian population that live alongside the Coventry Canal in the north part of the city. This one explains the importance of water in the Hindu religion.

The Oxford Canal

Brindley's Grand Cross of canals was completed eighteen years after his death when the Oxford Canal finally reached its destination with the River Thames at Oxford in 1790. The original canal between Hawkesbury Junction and Oxford was 90 miles long but Brindley's meandering, contour-hugging waterway led to severe bottlenecks and time-wasting when the canal was busy. To speed up trade, fourteen miles was lopped off the northern section above Braunston during the 1930s by straightening out the loops with a new canal. The winding southern section remained the same and is today one of the most popular cruising waterways in the country.

Right: Napton Locks on the Oxford Canal. The canal blends in so perfectly with the landscape it is hard to believe you are looking at an artificial waterway. Some changes have been made next to the towpath since this photograph was taken in 1974 but mostly this timeless scene remains unspoilt.

The windmill on Napton Hill overlooks Napton Locks and the Oxford Canal. The first windmill on Napton Hill was built in the middle of the 16th century. Clay was moved by boat from the extensive quarries that bit into the hillside. There is a beautiful view of the surrounding countryside from beneath the windmill (see opposite).

Cropredy Lock on the Oxford Canal. On the 29th June 1644 a furious battle took place at Cropredy Bridge between Cromwell's army and a Royalist force during the Civil War. Both factions were well matched, each with around 9,000 men on horse or on foot. A plaque on the river bridge commemorates the battle. In more recent times, Cropredy is host to the Fairport Convention Music Festival that takes place on the second weekend in August attracting 20,000 music fans.

Above: The village church at Shipton-on-Cherwell predates the Oxford Canal by several centuries. On Christmas Eve 1874 there was a railway accident when a crowded train left the track and fell into the canal. 34 people were killed and 64 injured. This charming village is just a few miles north of Oxford close to Woodstock and Blenheim Palace, birthplace of Sir Winston Churchill.

Narrowboats on the Oxford Canal at Braunston near the junction with the Grand Union Canal. This section of the Oxford Canal between Braunston and Napton Junction is shared with the Grand Union Canal. Braunston became a place where working boat families congregated because of the carrying companies, boatyards and also to buy supplies. Braunston church was where they often married and buried their dead. Many of the old working boats and their traditions can be seen at an annual boat rally parade at Braunston.

Chesterfield Canal

The black and white photo shows the Pickford's Warehouse at Worksop on the Chesterfield Canal in June 1973. Boats using the covered arch could load and unload directly from the warehouse.

Below: The same view twenty years later in 1993 shows the warehouse converted into a pub with an adjoining supermarket car park. The building has undergone further changes but it is still operating as a pub. It has become part of the 100 British Waterways Waterside Pubs Partnership scheme announced in 2005. Worksop is at the edge of that part of Sherwood Forest known as the Dukeries. Three large estates at Clumber, Welbeck and Thoresby are all close to Worksop. Clumber Park and Thorseby Park are open to the public but Welbeck is an army college and not open to visitors.

The Chesterfield Canal is an isolated waterway only connected to the rest of the system by the tidal River Trent. Originally surveyed by Brindley, construction of the 45-mile canal began in 1771 and took six years to complete. At first It was a very successful waterway, but the 3102 yard long Norwood Tunnel proved unstable from the outset. It was one of the longest canal tunnels ever built in Britain, and eventually had to be closed in 1907 after the roof collapsed. The canal fell into decline and the section between Worksop and Chesterfield became derelict. Only the efforts of volunteers and the Retford and Worksop Boat Club kept the rest of the canal open. The canal has been now been restored as far as Norwood Tunnel and work is progressing at the Chesterfield end.

Below: The Chesterfield Canal at Cinderhill near Shireoaks. This beautiful section between Worksop and Norwood Tunnel has only recently been restored after years of dereliction.

The Pennine Canals
'Among those dark satanic mills'

The Leeds and Liverpool Canal at Burnley photographed in
May 1972. Several of the mills in the picture have since been
demolished – one after a fire. Despite the loss, this section
of canal in Burnley has become a heritage trail and is being
promoted as the Weavers' Triangle. Burnley also has an
impressive 60 foot embankment that carries the canal
across part of the town and is almost a mile in length.

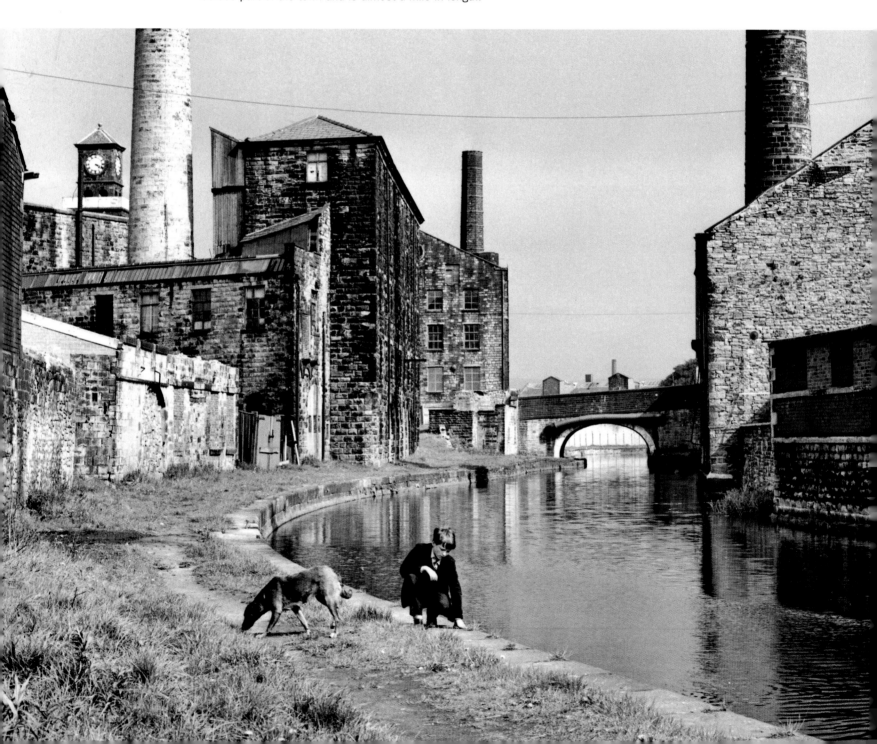

Three canals cross the Pennine watershed. On each side of the hills they pass through old industrial towns whose prosperity was made in the wool and cotton trade. The canals enabled the mills to be supplied with essential raw materials and provided an outlet to the ports at Liverpool and Hull. Between them the three canals required 260 locks in various sizes to allow boats to pass over their summit levels in the high hills. One of the canals also needed the longest canal tunnel ever built in Britain at Standedge.

Two of the canals – the Rochdale Canal and the Huddersfield Narrow Canal – eventually succumbed to economic pressure. They were closed and became derelict. Only the Leeds and Liverpool Canal, which is the longest and the oldest of the three, managed to survive. The Rochdale and Huddersfield Canals have since been restored to full navigation.

The locks were hard work for working boatmen in bygone days but the superb Pennine moorland scenery has become a great attraction for today's pleasure boaters.

Below: Greenberfield Top Lock on the Pennine section of the Leeds and Liverpool Canal. At 127 miles, the Leeds and Liverpool is the longest canal in Britain. On the Lancashire side it passes through old mill towns like Blackburn, Burnley and Wigan, with Bingley and Skipton on the Yorkshire side.

Below left: Apart from the five staircase locks at Bingley, there are several groups of three staircase locks on the Yorkshire side of the Leeds and Liverpool Canal. Newlay Locks near Bramley on the outskirts of Leeds are attractively set in woodland by a country park.

Bingley Five Rise raise the Leeds and Liverpool Canal 60 feet by a series of staircase locks in which one chamber leads into the next without an intervening pound. This means that the top gates of the lower lock become the bottom gates of the one above. An attendant lock-keeper is at hand to help confused boaters negotiate the flight.

Below: Daisyfield Mill by the Leeds and Liverpool Canal at Blackburn was built as a corn mill in 1870. In later years it was a wallpaper factory and has now been converted to offices and a television studio. The canal in the Blackburn area was once flanked by mills with industries that included paper making, cotton, flour and oat crushing. Terraced houses built for mill workers still remain by the canal in many northern towns like Blackburn. Whole families including children as young as ten years old would work long hours in the mill at the bottom of the street.

Above: Trencherfield Mill at Wigan once produced cotton but is now part of the 'Wigan Pier Heritage experience'. It still has a massive working steam engine that once powered textile machines on five floors operating 7,000 spindles. This unlikely part of the Leeds and Liverpool Canal in Wigan has become a major tourist attraction in the North West.

The Rochdale Canal in Todmorden when it was derelict in November 1973. The canal has since been restored but every building in this picture has been demolished. The Rochdale Canal was fully operational by 1804 which was seven years before its Huddersfield Narrow Canal neighbour. Commercially it was very successful because its broad locks allowed quite large vessels to cross the Pennine hills. Its problem lay in its very short summit level with inadequate water supplies to maintain busy traffic through 92 locks.

Left: A long flight of locks takes the Rochdale Canal through Todmorden up to the short summit level.

Below: Shade Lock on the Rochdale Canal at Todmorden. In the background is Gauxholme Viaduct which was built in 1841 by George Stephenson for the Manchester and Leeds Railway. A long retaining wall between railway and canal, locally called 'The Great Wall of Todmorden', has four million bricks.

Todmorden became prosperous by cotton spinning and weaving. It once had the largest weaving shed in the world.

This area of Calderdale has reported a number of UFO (Unidentified Flying Objects) sightings in recent years. In 1980 a local policeman was convinced he had a close encounter with an alien spaceship and took tests under hypnosis to prove he wasn't lying.

Below: The last commercial boat to pass through the Rochdale Canal was narrow boat *Alice* carrying 20 tons of wire from Sowerby Bridge to Manchester in 1937. The canal became derelict, with bridges lowered and culverted and locks converted into weirs. There were plans to fill in several urban stretches which had become rubbish dumps. The lock in the picture was taken in November 1973 on the western side of the canal. The first great clean up of the canal led by voluntary labour began in 1972 and the canal was finally reopened throughout in 2002.

Above: The line of the Rochdale Canal just south of Rochdale had to be re-routed because of the nearby motorway. Consequently, a brand new lock had to be built. The picture shows the lock under construction in May 2002 only two months before the entire canal was officially reopened.

Right: Tuel Lane Lock
was opened in 1996 and
replaced two derelict
structures in the centre
of Sowerby Bridge. It is
almost 20 feet deep which
makes it the deepest canal
lock in the country.
The lock is manned by a
resident lock-keeper so
boaters should check times
of operation.

A short tunnel under
the main road was also
required to reconnect the
Rochdale Canal to the
Calder and Hebble
Navigation. Sowerby Bridge
Basin has moorings and a
boatyard surrounded by a
collection of superb stone
warehouses. Sowerby
Bridge, with its numerous
pubs and restaurants,
makes an ideal stopping
place for boaters attempting
the South Pennine Cruising
Ring.

Left: Moorings at Warland beneath high moorland hills on the Rochdale Canal summit. These moorings are near Steanor Bottom Toll House where two Turnpike Roads ended. An interesting list of 19th century tolls can be seen on a plaque at the toll house.

Below: Surrounded by high hills, Hebden Bridge epitomises the rugged, stone built Northern mill town. The 'double-decker' houses that once housed mill workers can still be seen clinging to the steep hillside. Hebden Bridge and Heptonstall became prosperous for the production of corduroy and worsted textiles. It also became notorious in the mid-18th century for the Cragg Vale Coiners. Cragg Vale was an isolated village near Hebden Bridge where 'King' David Hartley and his gang of counterfeiters made gold coins of such quality that they went undetected for several years. The story ended in the betrayal of David Hartley and the murder of an Excise Officer. Hartley was hanged at York in April 1770 and is buried at Heptonstall.

Diggle Locks on the Huddersfield Narrow Canal. Only 20 miles long, it was the shortest of the Pennine canals. Even so there were still 74 narrow locks and Britain's longest canal tunnel to negotiate. The canal suffered from bad workmanship in its original construction, leaving it with flooding problems in later years. Not surprisingly these problems coupled with difficulties in negotiating Standedge Tunnel and competition from the railway brought the waterway into decline. It was abandoned after the Second World War but restored in 2001. Diggle Locks can be found on the western side of Standedge Tunnel as the canal descends through the Lancashire mill towns to Manchester.

Left: The Huddersfield Narrow Canal at Saddleworth Viaduct near Uppermill.

Below: The entrance to Standedge Tunnel at Marsden looks like a mousehole underneath the towering Standedge Fell. At 5,415 feet it is by far the longest canal tunnel in Britain. In the days before powered boats, boatmen had to 'leg' the boats through the tunnel by 'walking' them along the tunnel wall, thereby pushing the boats through. Since the tunnel was restored in 2001. Only electric boats are allowed to penetrate the interior because of poor ventilation.

Right: Beneath this mill at Huddersfield is a bizarre lifting bridge called Locomotive Bridge that looks as if it was made out of Meccano pieces. The mill is close to the former transhipment basin where boats had to transfer cargoes from the wide Huddersfield Broad Canal to the Narrow trans-Pennine waterway.

Above: Jack James photographed outside his cottage at Stoke Bruerne in June 1973. Mr James was a working boatman who later became a lock-keeper. His collection of waterway memorabilia was the foundation for the country's first Canal Museum at Stoke Bruerne. He died aged 78 in September 1974.

Below: A pair of coal carrying narrowboats outside the Boat Inn at Stoke Bruerne in 1973. The interior of a narrow boat cabin was a masterpiece in the utilisation of space. Less than 7 feet wide, 9 feet long and under 6 feet high, boatmen's families would live, eat and sleep within these confines.

The London Road

The London Road was the name given by working boatmen to the Grand Junction Canal. It was built between Braunston and the River Thames at Brentford as a quicker alternative route to London than the meandering, narrow locked Oxford Canal. It also avoided transhipment to Thames barges at Oxford followed by a long journey down river to London. The Grand Junction had wide locks, two long tunnels and an aqueduct over the River Great Ouse. It cut the previous journey by 60 miles.

A new route to Birmingham was established by the building of the Napton, Warwick and Birmingham Canals. Another connection to the Grand Junction was made to Leicester and then by the canalised River Soar to the Trent. All these waterways and their branches amalgamated in 1929 becoming the Grand Union Canal.

Right: Steam powered narrow boat *President* with butty boat *Kildare* in Stoke Bruerne Top Lock. The crew are dressed in traditional boatmen's clothes. The Canal Museum, housed in a former grain warehouse, can be seen by the trees in the background on the right of the picture.

Left: Braunston village, about two miles to the north west of Daventry in Northamptonshire, is the hub of the inland waterway system south of Birmingham. Situated at the junction of the Grand Union and Oxford Canals, it has long been a gathering place for working narrow boats. The picture shows narrow boats at a working boat rally at Braunston in June 2000.

Below: Narrow boats *Alperton* and *Widgeon* carrying an experimental cargo of Massey Ferguson boxed tractors on the Grand Union Canal near Ivinghoe in February 1974. The boats went to Brentford where the tractors were loaded on to Thames lighters before being exported to South Africa from London Docks.

Right: Hatton Bottom Lock, with its pretty lock cottage, is at the foot of the Hatton lock flight on the outskirts of Warwick.

Below: The daunting sight of 21 wide locks striding up the hillside at Hatton has made many a boatman quiver in his boots. It requires around 50,000 gallons of water to fill one of these Grand Union Canal locks, so a boat travelling up the flight releases a prodigious amount of water. Some water is saved by using the side pounds next to each lock which act as a reservoir. This view looking down the flight towards Warwick is taken from near the top of the locks.

Below: Blisworth on the Grand Union Canal is the third longest navigable tunnel in Britain. It opened in 1805 and is wide enough for two narrow boats to pass each other inside. There is no towpath so boats had to be 'legged' through in the days before powered craft. Professional 'leggers' used to work boats through the tunnel - at a price! During the early 1980s the tunnel was closed because of structural problems and needed to be re-lined. The picture shows work on the inside of the tunnel in October 1983.

Above: A narrowboat enters the north end of Blisworth Tunnel. Waterproof clothing is recommended for steerers, especially after wet weather, as water pours down the ventilation shafts above the tunnel.

Above: After miles of lock-free cruising, the ten staircase locks at Foxton can be a shock to the boater. They are arranged in two sets of five locks with a passing place between. In 1900 a steam-driven inclined plane was built to bypass the traffic bottleneck at Foxton Locks. It lasted only a few years before closing as it was expensive to operate and often broke down. Today, Foxton Locks are very popular with visitors who come to picnic and watch the boats.

Left: In its southern section, the Leicester Canal meanders through peaceful farming countryside.

Below: The Leicester branch of the Grand Union Canal at Crick. This is the beautiful setting for an annual boating festival at the end of May in a nearby marina. Cracks Hill, which was a Roman station, has superb views from its summit. Crick and its neighbour Husbands Bosworth both have long canal tunnels which were built in order to maintain a 20 mile level pound between the lock flights at Foxton and Watford (Northants).

Sandiacre Lock on the Erewash Canal near Nottingham. Although the canal was built to serve the Nottinghamshire coafields, it also provided an important outlet for the lace mills by the canal at Long Eaton and Sandiacre. At its southern end the Erewash Canal begins its journey at a watery crossroads by the River Trent. Great Northern Basin at Langley Mill is the northern terminus where the canal connected to the now disused Nottingham and Cromford Canals.

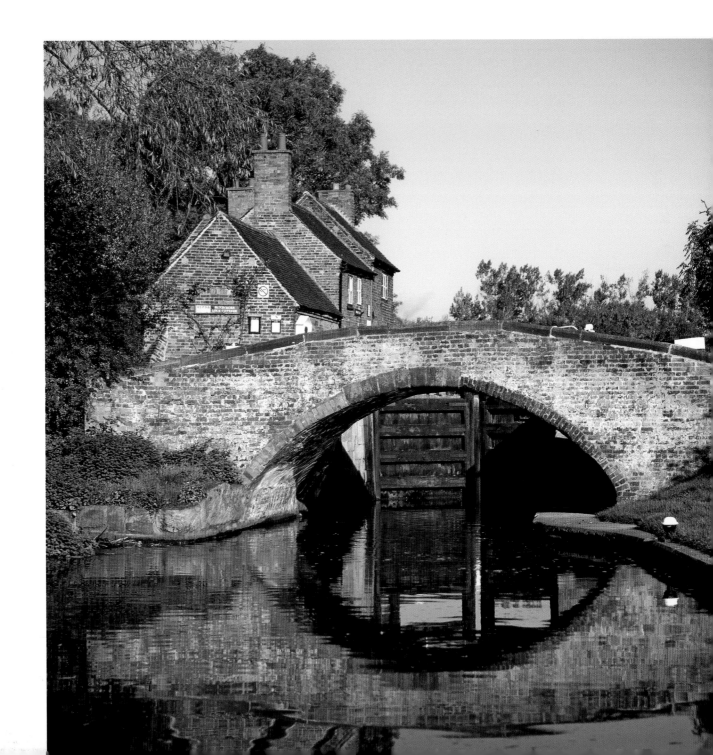

The London Canals

The Grand Junction Canal reached the Thames at Brentford in 1894 but was still some distance from the Docks and central London. The first canal to reach the centre of London was the Paddington Branch of the Grand Junction Canal which opened in July 1801. The Regent's Canal connected Paddington to the River Thames at Limehouse in 1820. The Paddington Canal was responsible for much of the industrial and social development of north west London. All these waterways were intensely busy in their commercial heyday, which lasted well into the second half of the twentieth century. There were some canals south of the river but these have all disappeared under urban development. There are many changes on the existing canals north of the river with huge developments at Paddington and Brentford.

Right: Boating on the Regent's Canal at London Zoo. In the background is Lord Snowdon's Aviary. This is, without doubt, one of the finest stretches of urban waterway in the country. The best way to visit London Zoo is to take the Waterbus from Little Venice.

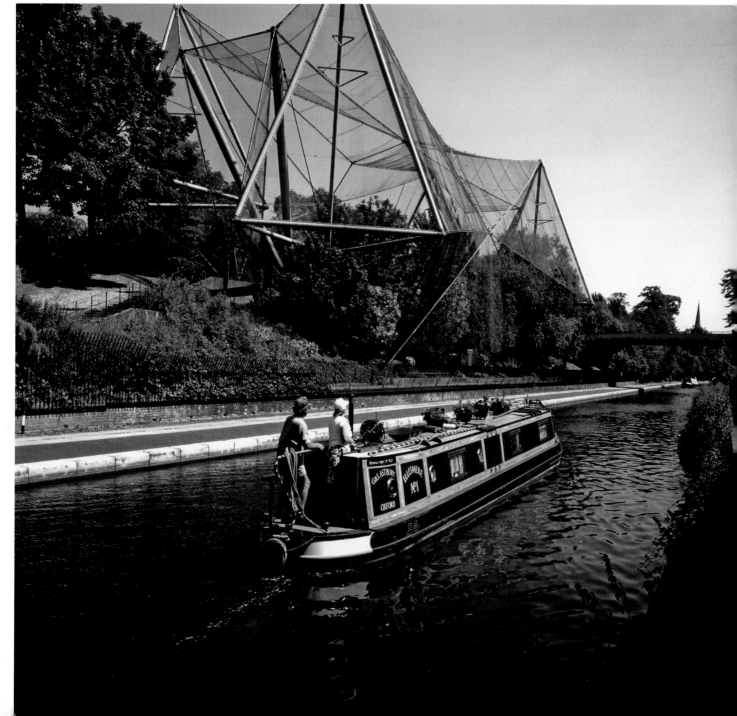

Port-A-Bella Dock on the Paddington Canal at Ladbroke Grove was once a council disposal point for domestic rubbish. The rubbish was taken by boats to fill holes left by quarrying around West Drayton on the outskirts of West London. In later years it became a restaurant and has been used as the headquarters of a prominent record company. Port-A-Bella Dock is at Ladbroke Grove close to the starting point for the Notting Hill Carnival that takes place annually at the end of August.

Left: Three Mills at Bow by the River Lee Navigation in East London has some of the finest waterside buildings in London. The House Mill was built in 1776 and is the oldest and largest tidal mill in Britain. The Clock Mill was built later in 1817. Tidal mills work by allowing tidal water to flow upstream by holding ebbing water by the use of floodgates. The gates open when the downstream water level drops and the onrushing water turns the mill wheels.

Below: Camden Lock, with its cosmopolitan market, is one of the best known places on London's canals. From here you can take a trip boat to Little Venice via London Zoo. All the Regent's Canal locks were duplicated because the canal was once so busy with commercial traffic. The locks in the picture are actually known as Hampstead Road Locks and they are the only paired locks still in use.

Left: In September 2004 Brentford Depot had become a huge building site. Most of the warehouses have gone and are being replaced by new houses, hotels, restaurants and waterside bars.

Below: Brentford Transhipment Depot was busy up to the mid-1980s when most commercial water traffic had finally ended. Afterwards the warehouses remained active but goods were mostly moved by road transport. This picture was taken in 1965 when the depot was still thriving and bustling with barges and narrowboats.

Left: A pleasant afternoon taking tea on a waterside veranda above the Regent's Canal at Maida Hill near Little Venice.

Below: The Canalway Cavalcade is an annual event during the first weekend of May at Little Venice. The water is packed with boats and the quayside has booths selling everything from food and books to plants for the garden. Little Venice is the starting place for passenger trip boats to London Zoo and Camden Lock. The island in the centre of the pool is named after the poet Robert Browning who lived in this area. It is possible that the name Little Venice originated with Browning who loved Venice where he died in 1889. From Little Venice it is a short walk to Paddington Waterside (formerly Paddington Basin) to see Europe's biggest modern waterside development.

Below: Regent's Canal Dock, now known as Limehouse Basin, in May 1968. The vehicles lined up on the jetty are waiting to be loaded for export. The quaysides are busy with sea-going coasters and barges. The buildings in the background have all now disappeared as part of the Docklands development. The photograph was taken from a railway viaduct which was then disused but is now part of the Docklands Light Railway.

Left: Limehouse Basin today has a large expanse of water devoted to moorings for a wide miscellany of canal and river craft. It is the home of the Cruising Association.

Right: A small sailing ship passing Canary Wharf in London Docklands.

London's River

Left: The Millennium Dome by the Thames on the Greenwich Peninsula. One of London's more controversial buildings of recent years, its future as an entertainment and sports arena seems assured. Expected to seat over 20,000 people, it will probably be a venue in London's 2012 Olympic Games.

Below: Canary Wharf and its satellite buildings viewed from across the Thames by the Millennium Dome.

Below: A flotilla of boats leaves St Katharine's Dock into the Pool of London by Tower Bridge. St Katharine's Dock was built by Thomas Telford and was opened in 1828. The warehouses still remain and have been converted into apartments and shops. Thames sailing barges can often be seen in the dock. They were built for cargo carrying and continued to do so as late as the 1970s. Now they can be seen in full sail at regattas especially in the Thames estuary and at Maldon in Essex.

Right: The Queen Elizabeth II suspension bridge carries the southbound M25 motorway over the Thames at Dartford. It is the last crossing place across the river before the estuary. Northbound traffic has to go underground into tunnels. The bridge was opened in October 1991 and at busy times can carry 100,000 vehicles in a day.

Right: The tideway at Hammersmith in September 1980. This section of river is part of the annual Oxford and Cambridge Varsity Boat Race. In 1870 the original bridge at Hammersmith almost collapsed when 12,000 people crowded on to it to watch the Boat Race. This bridge, built in 1827, was later demolished and the present structure designed by Sir Joseph Bazalgette was erected in 1887.

Sir Joseph Bazalgette (1819–1891) was the engineering genius who built the Thames Embankment in Central London following the cholera epidemic during the Big Stink of 1858. He also constructed London's first sewer network which was completed in 1866 and is still in use today.

Left: Now surrounded by luxury hotels and smart apartments, Chelsea Harbour was once a humble coal wharf. The marina plays host to some very expensive river and sea going craft.

Below: Commercial traffic on the Thames at Southwark. In the background is the Tate Modern art gallery in the former Bankside Power Station. Also to be seen is the Globe Theatre. The Millennium footbridge between St Paul's Cathedral and the Tate Modern had a shaky start when it was deemed unsafe. Now strengthened, it has become a popular landmark over the river at Southwark. Now a continual public footpath is open from Westminster Bridge to Bermondsey.

Below: Tower Bridge was designed by Sir Horace Jones and opened in 1894, seven years after his death. It was designed as a bascule bridge because of its proximity to the London docks when its central part would be lifted several times a day for passing ships. Although the docks have gone, the bridge is raised around 500 times a year for tall vessels. The high level walkway was the haunt of prostitutes and pickpockets and was closed in 1910.

The walkway has now been reopened to the public as part of the Tower Bridge Experience. The Girl on a Dolphin statue is by David Wynne and was erected here in 1973.

Royal River

The Thames at Laleham during a period of winter flooding in January 1994. A new flood diversion channel known as the Jubilee River opened in June 2002 between Maidenhead and Windsor. January 2003 saw the worst floods on the river since 1947. The new channel came into use and avoided serious flooding at Maidenhead and Windsor. Some controversy arose when residents in the Wraysbury area complained that the new flood prevention scheme was actually increasing the flooding risk in their part of the river downstream.

Above: The thickly wooded Cliveden Reach on one of the finest sections of the River Thames. The present Cliveden House was built in 1851 on the site of an
earlier one that burnt down. It was bought by the Astor family in 1893 and became a fashionable place for prominent figures in politics and the arts known as 'The Cliveden Set'. It was the location for a famous political scandal that nearly toppled the Government during the early 1960s. The house is now owned by the National Trust who lease it to a hotel group. Cliveden House has splendid gardens and woodland walks with wonderful views across the river from its lofty position.

Right: '
A tranquil part of the River Thames at Lower Shiplake. The village has literary connections with Alfred Lord Tennyson who married here in 1850 and George Orwell who lived here as a boy.

'Sweet Thames! Run softly, till I end my song.'
Edmund Spenser.

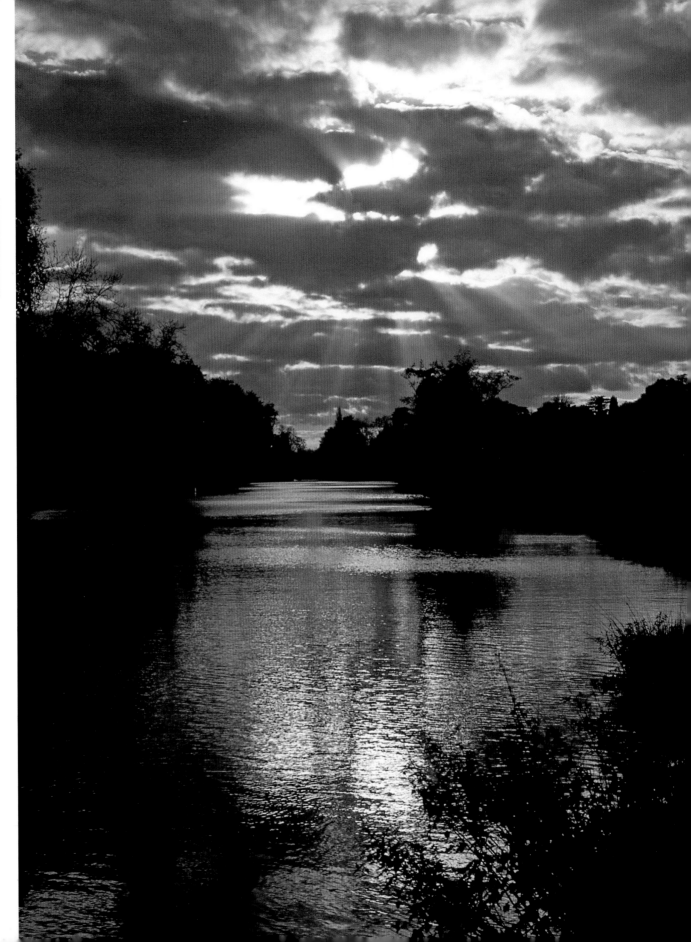

Clifton Hampden Bridge has a medieval appearance
although it was actually built in the Victorian Era. Jerome K
Jerome wrote part of his classic Thames novel *Three Men in a
Boat* while residing in the nearby Barley Mow Inn. The local
church is perched on a rocky outcrop overlooking the river.
In its churchyard is a memorial to Sergeant William Dykes who
accidentally fired the first shot at the Battle of Waterloo and was
subsequently court martialled by the Duke of Wellington.

Left: Children play on a sand bar at the edge of the river while their grandparents enjoy the summer sunshine. This idyllic scene is by the Thames near Marlow.

Below: Winter Hill near Marlow was a favourite place of Charles Dickens who loved to climb the hill and enjoy the extensive views over the Thames Valley. It is believed Kenneth Grahame used Winter Hill for the Wild Wood in his book *Wind in the Willows*.

Left: The infant River Thames near Kemble in Gloucestershire, only a mile from the river's source at Thames Head.

Below: A canal boat turns at the end of navigation on the Upper Thames at Inglesham. Behind the willow trees is the entrance to the long derelict Thames and Severn Canal. The first of several round houses typical to this canal can be seen by the first lock.

Right: The River Avon at Offenham. Some of the locks on the River Avon were renamed after benefactors during the period of restoration. George Billington Lock is the first one on the Upper Avon and was built in the winter of 1969.

Shakespeare's Avon

The derelict southern section of the Stratford-upon-Avon Canal and the defunct Lower Avon Navigation were both restored and reopened in 1964. In each case voluntary labour was responsible for the successful campaign to reopen these beautiful waterways against officialdom who in the main would have preferred to have left them closed. It took another ten years to complete the restoration of the Upper Avon which opened up the now popular Avon Cruising Ring. The highlight of the journey is, of course, Stratford-upon-Avon with its many Shakespearean connections.

Below: The 17th century Eckington Bridge over the River Avon. There are glorious views as the river twists and winds around Bredon Hill in the Vale of Evesham.

Left: Split bridges are one of the distinctive features of the Stratford-upon-Avon Canal. Two cast-iron cantilevered sections leave a gap that allows the boat horse's rope to pass through a fixed bridge without being unhitched.

Below; Lapworth Locks on the Southern Stratford-upon-Avon Canal. The beautiful scenery on this canal has made it one of the most popular waterways on the inland navigation system.

Below: Bancroft Basin at Stratford-upon-Avon is where boats can stop to visit the town. The waterside is thronged with visitors from all over the world who take a special interest in watching boats pass through the lock between the basin and the River Avon. Shakespeare's birthplace, a 16th century half-timbered house with a beautiful cottage garden, is just a short walk from the canal. A Shakespeare memorial statue shows the bard looking over the canal basin surrounded by characters from his plays. The Royal Shakespeare Theatre is by the River Avon and the 15th century Clopton Bridge is now a footbridge over the river.

Below: A branch canal from the Grand Union joins the Stratford-upon-Avon Canal at Kingswood Junction. This provides an alternative route into Birmingham from the south. During the years of decline on the canals the northern Stratford Canal was never shut down like its southern counterpart. Keeping the canal open became a cause celebre when in 1947 the author Tom Rolt applied his right of navigation and forced the railway company to jack up a fixed bridge at Tunnel Lane, Kings Norton. The point was made with maximum press coverage and the action drew a large crowd who cheered Mr Rolt as he sailed past the obstacle.

A barrel-roofed lock cottage at Lowsonford on the southern Stratford-upon-Avon Canal. This is one of the few cottages of this type that remain unspoilt. Others have added extensions that are totally out of keeping with the original building. The reason for building the cottages in this way has never been properly explained. The theory that they were constructed by builders who only knew how to build bridges and tunnels is surely apocryphal.

Lowsonford is an attractive village that has a pub with a large waterside garden. The building of the Fleur de Lys pub was created from a former blacksmith's shop and a morgue. In later years the pub became famous for production of meat pies.

The Changing Face of Birmingham

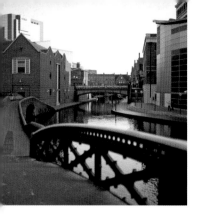

Below: The view from Old Turn Junction towards Broad Street in August 1973. This part of Birmingham had become very run-down and most of the old factories were derelict. Within 20 years every building in this picture had gone including the church that stood above Broad Street Tunnel. The only things that remained were the footpath bridges.

Left: The same view from Old Turn Junction in 2005. The towpath bridges are all that remain from the picture taken 1973. On the left of the picture is the International Convention Centre and a new pub. The National Sea Life Centre and Brindley Place are to the right. The National Indoor Arena is behind the camera position. In the canal's commercial heyday, Old Turn Junction would have been congested with working boats resting up before heading to the Birmingham Main Line Canal, or to the Grand Junction Canal or the Worcester and Birmingham Canal.

Below: Brindley Place has become the vibrant centre for Birmingham's night life with waterside restaurants and night clubs. During the day, it is a popular place to spend an hour sitting at a café or bar watching the boats go past.

Right: The trip boat *Jericho* waits for passengers outside the International Convention Centre. The Convention Centre opened in 1991 and has seven halls including Symphony Hall, home of the City of Birmingham Symphony Orchestra.

A passenger trip boat t Old Turn Junction with he National Indoor Arena n the background. The ndoor Arena has become n important place to stage orting and music events om tennis tournaments to he Eurovision Song ontest. It opened in 991 and can seat 0,000 people.

Above: In 2004 boats in Gas Street Basin are dominated by the Hyatt Hotel's glass monolith.

Right: Birmingham's Gas Street Basin in October 1975. Gas Street Basin still remained in its own private world, enclosed by warehouses and old canal buildings. At that time, the Hyatt Hotel and all today's modern buildings were a mere glint in the developer's eye. Now one side of the basin has been opened out and a pub called the James Brindley sits on that side.

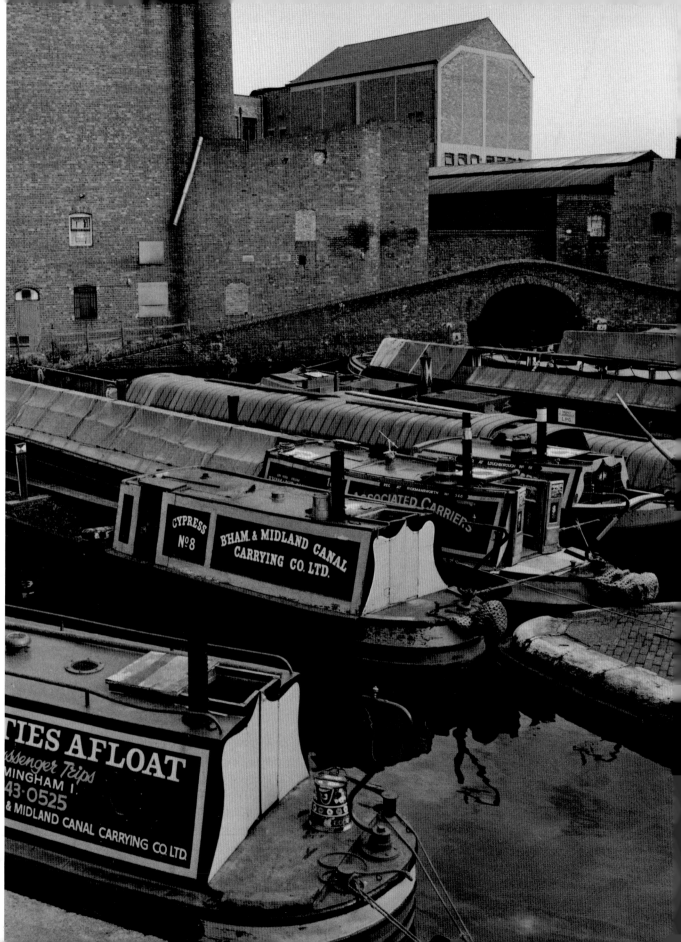

The Back of the Map

The Back of the Map was a term used by the working boatmen to describe the Dudley and Stourbridge Canals. These highly industrialised waterways connected the Staffs and Worcester Canal to the rest of the Black Country Canals. Three long tunnels were required to pierce the Rowley Hills; Netherton Tunnel is the only one still in regular use by motor boats. Dudley Tunnel, although restored, is only used by electrically powered craft from the nearby Black Country Museum. This is because of inadequate ventilation inside the tunnel. Lapal Tunnel that once connected The Dudley Canal to the Worcester and Birmingham Canal was never stable and eventually the roof collapsed forcing the tunnel to close in 1917.

eans Foundry on the irmingham Main Line anal at Tipton Green. he foundry was a target r enemy bombers in the econd World War but they issed! The foundry is still ere and still in business. can be seen close by the lack Country Museum.

Right: Delph Locks
at Brierley Hill carry the
Dudley Canal down to a
junction with the Stourbridge
Canal at the bottom of the
hill. When the picture was
taken in August 1973, there
was a coal mine with its
attendant slag heaps at the
bottom of the flight.

Above: Compare the black
and white picture with the
colour photo taken 25
years later that shows the
colliery has gone and has
been replaced by a housing
estate.

Windmill End Junction on the Dudley Canal is a watery cross-road spanned by a series of delightful and elegant cast iron bridges. They were cast at Horseley Iron Works in the Black Country. The ruins of Cobb's Engine House stands close by the entrance to Netherton Tunnel. Built around 1830, it once pumped water from one of the many mines dotted around these hillsides. It remains as a stark emblem to the region's industrial past. Now the Rowley Hills provide a welcome touch of greenery in an intensely built-up area.

The Black Country Museum at Dudley describes itself as having '26 acres of Living History to Explore'. It includes a Black Country Village built around an old canal arm and the approach to Dudley Tunnel. One of the main visitor attractions is an underground voyage into the caverns of the Dudley Tunnel by electric boat.

Left: A village street at the museum leading down to the Boat Dock.

Above: The Black Country Museum under construction in 1976. The bridge was moved here from its original place over the canal in Wolverhampton. In the picture contractors are securing the bridge in its present position.

Right: The same bridge in its permanent place at the entrance to the village.

Canals in Manchester

The Manchester Ship Canal was opened in 1894 and was the last major canal built in Britain. It runs for 36 miles from the tidal River Mersey at Eastham to Manchester. Manchester Docks at the head of the ship canal closed to commercial traffic in the early 1980s. It was redeveloped for housing, commerce and recreation and renamed Salford Quays. Present day attractions include the Imperial War Museum North and the Lowry Centre with its art gallery, theatre and restaurants. The Lowry Centre contains 300 paintings by the Manchester born artist who specialised in painting the local industrial scene with its 'matchstick men and matchstick cats and dogs'.

Below: The Victoria Building at Salford Quays looks like Manchester's answer to the Taj Mahal.

Left: The bridge at Dukinfield Junction at Ashton-under-Lyne in eastern Manchester. The bridge is the meeting place of three canals – the Ashton Canal from central Manchester, the Peak Forest Canal from Whaley Bridge and the Huddersfield Narrow Canal. The Portland Basin Industrial Museum is opposite the bridge where there is also a collection of vintage canal boats. The original warehouse was derelict for years following a disastrous fire in the 1970s. It was restored in 1999 as the Portland Basin Museum which houses industrial and community-based exhibits.

Below: Castle Quay at Castlefield in the centre of Manchester. This is where the Duke of Bridgewater's Canal ended its journey from the Duke's mines at Worsley. There are some splendid restored warehouses in this area which have been converted to new uses. In recent years, Castlefield has become Manchester's trendy centre for pubs, restaurants and night clubs.

The Ashton Canal at Ancoats Locks in Manchester.
This short urban canal in eastern Manchester has 18 locks in just over 6 miles. The main highlight of the journey is the City of Manchester Stadium by Beswick Locks where the 2002 Commonwealth Games were held. It is now the home of Manchester City Football Club. The Ashton Canal lay derelict and rubbish-filled for many years before being reopened in 1974. Although it is unlikely to win any prizes for its scenic beauty, it is nevertheless an integral part of the Cheshire Cruising Ring.

Right: The Peak Forest Canal clings to the hillside above the River Goyt Valley to the south east of Manchester. This section is at Strines which is between Marple and Whaley Bridge. Cargoes on the Peak Forest Canal once crossed the hills of the Peak District from Whaley Bridge to the Cromford Canal by means of the Cromford and High Peak Railway. Buxworth Basin was an important interchange point where tramways connected the canal with the Doveholes limestone quarries. After years of disuse, the basin is again navigable by boat and its limekilns have been restored.

Above: Albion Mills Lock on the Deansgate Flight, popularly known as the Rochdale Nine. These locks are part of the Rochdale Canal which at one end has a junction with the Ashton Canal at Ancoats and meets the Bridegwater Canal at the other. This last section of the Rochdale Canal is flanked by nightclubs, discos and restaurants

Canals in Wales

Below: Walkers on the wooded Monmouthshire and Brecon Canal near Llangynidr. Affectionately known as the 'Mon and Brec', this beautiful, isolated canal lies mostly within the Brecon Beacons National Park. This picture was taken in June 1972 shortly after the canal had been reopened for navigation.

Right: The Monmouthshire and Brecon Canal at Mamhila near Pontypool. Until recently Pontymoile Basin, two miles south of Mamhilad, was the southern limit of navigation on this canal. Now restorers have extended the navigation three miles toward Cwmbran. In time it is hoped to reach Newport which is 5 miles and 30 locks away.

Below: Llanfoist was the site of a tramroad over the Blorenge mountain where trucks brought their loads from limestone quarries. A second line linked the ironworks at Blaenavon with the canal wharf. The building to the right of the picture was once a warehouse with a loading wharf from the tramroad to the canal. It is hard to believe that this enchanted spot on the Monmouthshire and Brecon Canal was once a place of intense industrial activity.

Left: The Llangollen Canal is one of Britain's most popular cruising waterways. Sun Trevor Bridge near Llangollen, with its canalside pub, is a favourite stopping place for boaters. The mountain in the background has the remains of Castell Dinas Bran and overlooks the town of Llangollen. Castell Dinas Bran was built around 1260 and occupies the site of a former Iron Age hillfort. The poet William Wordsworth visited the ruin and afterwards wrote 'Relics of Kings, wreck of forgotten wars, to the winds abandoned and the prying stars'.

Below: A misty autumn morning in Llangollen. This bridge is on the final narrow section of canal before reaching the end of the navigation at the Horseshoe Falls. It was originally built as a feeder, bringing water from the River Dee to the canal and later made navigable. Llangollen is the home of the International Musical Eisteddfod that attracts performers and visitors from all over the world each July. It also has a steam railway that runs for 8 miles beside the River Dee.

Left: The disused Neath Canal near Swansea in South Wales is slowly being restored in short sections. A scheme to restore an aqueduct and three locks was given the go ahead in July 2005. This will extend navigation to about six miles along the beautiful Vale of Neath. The picture shows the trip boat *Thomas Dadford* on a restored section near Resolven in 1993.

Right: The Montgomery Canal connects to the Llangollen Canal at Welsh Frankton near Ellesmere. Boats moved limestone from the quarries along the route but otherwise it was a mainly agricultural waterway. Never profitable, it fell into disuse and became derelict. Six miles at the top of the canal have now been reopened along with a 12 mile section around Welshpool in the middle. That leaves an awkward 8 mile derelict section before the two halves can be reunited. The picture shows the canal at Buttington Wharf near Welshpool.

Canals in Scotland

View of the Caledonian Canal at Laggan Bridge. Opened in 1822, the Caledonian Canal follows the geological fault line of the Great Glen and makes it possible for sea going boats to avoid the hazardous journey around Scotland's northern coast. The construction provided work for thousands of Highlanders during a period of high unemployment. Built by Thomas Telford and considered by many as his masterpiece, the 60 mile long waterway has 22 miles of artificial canal linking 38 miles of natural lochs.

Below: Laggan Cut was the biggest obstacle in building the Caledonian Canal. Hundreds of workmen (known as navvies) spent over seven years digging out the channel with picks and shovels which was all that was available to them at that time. It all looks very natural now, but then it would have been a blot on the landscape similar to today's motorway construction.

Right: A pleasure craft leaves Laggan Locks and heads out into Loch Lochy.

...rquhart Castle on the ...ore of Loch Ness which ...part of the Caledonian ...nal. The nearby village ...Drumnadrochit is the ...urist centre for the ...endary Loch Ness ...onster. The first modern ...hting of the monster was ...1933 which sparked ...much interest and ...eculation. A Loch Ness ...estigation Bureau ...s set up in the 1960s ...investigate the phenomenon. ...meras were set up with ...derwater listening ...vices and sonar scan-...rs but no evidence of a ...onster was found. The ...th of the Loch Ness ...onster attracts thousands ...visitors each year and ...s spawned a thriving ...essie' industry in that ...rt of the Highlands.

...fishing boat shares a ...k with pleasure cruisers ...Banavie Locks near Fort ...liam. This magnificent ...ht of eight locks is ...pularly known as ...eptune's Staircase'. ...ere are more staircase ...ks at Inverness and Fort ...gustus. Staircase locks ...e more economical to ...ld than conventional lock ...hts which have a waiting ...ction between each ...amber. In practice they ...n become bottlenecks for ...ating traffic as passage ...ough them is very slow. ...e Bingley Five Rise ...cks on page 34.)

Built in 1809, the Crinan Canal cuts across the Kintyre Peninsula, avoiding a difficult 130 mile journey around the Kintyre. The canal is 9 miles long with 15 locks and runs from Ardrishaig to Crinan Harbour. The Clyde Puffers regularly used canal as a safe route between Glasgow and Inverness. The on the Puffers sang a song whose chorus sums up why the the Crinan Canal.

'Oh! The Crinan Canal for me,
I don't like the wild raging sea,
The big foaming breakers would give me the shakers,
Its the Crinan Canal for me.'

Right: Cairnbaan has four locks and is about half way along the Crinan Canal.

The construction of the Forth and Clyde Canal allowed sea-going coasters to reach Glasgow and to navigate across the middle of Scotland. It was very busy in its early days until railway competition and the closure of Grangemouth Docks to merchant shipping during World War I took away much of its regular traffic. In 1962 the canal was closed when the new A80 road forced the canal into a culvert at Castlecary. It stayed closed until 2001 when the waterway was reopened and reconnected to the Union Canal by the amazing Falkirk Wheel (see page 157) Auchinstarry below is regarded as one of the most scenic stretches on the 35 mile long canal.

Right: The 32 mile long Union Canal connects Edinburgh to the Forth and Clyde Canal via the Falkirk Wheel. It has no locks, and so remains on a level contour throughout its length. To achieve this preservation of water, a number of impressive aqueducts and one tunnel were constructed. The Almond Aqueduct is near Ratho on the outskirts of Edinburgh.

Below: Leamington Lift Bridge is near the Union Canal terminus in the centre of Edinburgh. From here it is only a short walk to Princes Street and Edinburgh Castle.

Below: Bowling Basin is the terminus for the Forth and Clyde Canal at the western edge of Glasgow. Two sea locks give access into the wide River Clyde. The basin is now used for pleasure craft mooring.

Right: The Forth and Clyde Canal between Bowling and Old Kilpatrick. Old Kilpatrick is reputed to be the birthplace of St Patrick who was driven to Ireland by the Devil who threw rocks at him. One of the rocks landed in the middle of the River Clyde so a navigation light was placed upon it and called St Patrick's Stone Light. The Erskine Bridge towers above the canal at Old Kilpatrick before crossing the River Clyde. It was opened in 1971 and provides an alternative route between the Highlands and the south by avoiding central Glasgow.

East Anglian Waterways

Left: The Norfolk Wherry was the traditional Norfolk Broads sailing boat originally used for trading. *Albion,* one of the last surviving wherries, is now available for hire, and on this occasion was out on a school cruise on the River Ant.

Below: A typical Broads scene with sailing boat, motor cruiser and windmill. This is at How Hill on the River Ant where there is a 365 acre study centre. The estate has reed beds, marsh, woodland and a lake together with three restored drainage mills and a marshman's cottage. The study centre is owned by the How Hill Trust who run residential field courses for children and young people. The River Ant is narrower than the other Broads rivers and is navigable for eight miles.

The Broads of Norfolk and Suffolk are a complex series of shallow lakes linked by navigable rivers. It is a flat landscape of marshes and reed beds providing habitats for a wide variety of wildlife. It is also the most popular boating area in Britain. The Broads were formed because of medieval peat diggings for use as fuel. The holes left behind filled up when water levels rose. In 1978, the Broads Authority was formed to look after the region, and in 1989 it was given the status of a National Park. The sailing boat in the picture is near Acle Bridge on the River Bure. Acle Bridge was once a favourite place for executing criminals. Local folklore claims to have seen ghosts dangling over the parapet of the bridge.

Below: Although it is open to navigation, the 20 mile long New Bedford River is tidal and was built as a flood relief channel. Most boats take the more interesting route along the Old River Ouse past Ely.

Right: St Ives Bridge on the River Great Ouse is a chantry chapel bridge. Chapels were built on bridges for the spiritual needs of travellers who could give thanks after a long and arduous journey. They were called chantry chapels because masses were sung for the wellbeing of travellers and for the souls of victims of highway violence. They were common in the Middle Ages but most of them have disappeared over the years, leaving just four examples. They can be found at Wakefield, Rotherham, Bradford-on-Avon and at St Ives. This one was built in 1414, replacing a previous wooden structure.

The octagonal lantern tower of Ely Cathedral makes it visible for miles across the flat landscape of the Fens. Originally a Saxon church, it became a cathedral in 1109 at the time of William the Conqueror. It was built from limestone quarried at Barnack near Stamford in Lincolnshire, and is one of the finest examples of Romanesque architecture. Oliver Cromwell closed it for ten years and used it as stables for his cavalry horses. The cathedral is noted for its stained glass windows and contains a Stained Glass Museum. The Priors Door is an excellent example of Norman craftsmanship.

Stretham Old Engine was built in 1831 and was one of many steam powered drainage engines in the Fens. It pumped water from reclaimed land that was below sea level. The steam engine worked until 1941 when it was replaced by diesel power. The old engine has been preserved along with its tools in the pumping house which is open for public viewing. Stretham Old Engine is by the River Great Ouse a few miles south of Ely.

The twin Fenland villages of Upwell and Outwell sit on the daffodil-clad banks of the old course of the River Nene. Hereward the Wake lived here for a while after his defeat by the Normans. Originally called Welle, it was then the longest village in Britain. The villages assumed their present names when they were split.

The Round House at Chalford on the Thames and Severn Canal. These conical roofed lock cottages are only found on this waterway and no-one knows why they were built this way. Five of them have survived on the Thames and Severn.

A misty morning on the Thames and Severn Canal at Thrupp near Stroud. Over 70 years have passed since this section of the Thames and Severn Canal at Stantons Bridge near Stroud last saw a boat passing through. Although restoration is well under way, there are many locks to be rebuilt. Another major restoration problem is returning the navigation to Brimscombe Port where the canal has been built over for offices and car parks.

Western Canals

The restoration of the derelict Thames and Severn and Stroudwater Navigation is a massive task. Altogether there are 36 miles of waterway comprising 57 locks and a long leaky tunnel at Sapperton. The Thames and Severn, beset with water supply problems, finally closed in 1933. The Stroudwater Navigation lasted for another 21 years, before it, too, capitulated. Now reunited as the Cotswold Canals, it is just a question of how long and how much it will cost to restore these astonishingly beautiful waterways. The Cotswold Canal Trust, with over 5,000 members in 2005, was formed to promote the reopening of the canals.

Below: The Stroudwater Navigation at Stonehouse. St Cyr's Church looks over a short section of restored waterway.

Left: The Gloucester and Sharpness Canal at Frampton-on-Severn in Gloucestershire. Built as a ship canal, it is 16 miles long between Gloucester Docks and the River Severn at Sharpness Docks. It features distinctive bridge-keepers' cottages fronted with Doric porticoes and passes close to the Wildfowl Centre at Slimbridge.

Below: Gloucester Docks has become a popular centre for visitors. It is hard to believe that the superb old warehouses were once threatened with demolition because they were in such poor condition. Now one of them houses the National Waterways Museu and others have been converted to a variety of uses.

Left: The Wilts and Berks Canal at Dauntsey. This 50 mile long canal has been derelict for over a hundred years and much of its urban sections have been built over. Despite this The Wilts and Berks Canal Trust are gaining support for its eventual return to navigation and work parties are regularly engaged on restoration.

Below: Lord Rolle's Aqueduct over the River Torridge in North Devon. Lord Rolle built his six mile canal between Torrington and Bideford In 1823. The most impressive feature was this three-arched aqueduct. The canal has long gone but the aqueduct remains in good condition. It supports the driiveway to Beam House which once belonged to the Rolle family and is now an adventure holiday centre.

Southern Waterways

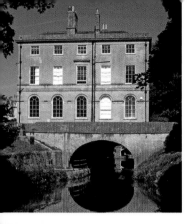

Below: Pulteney Bridge over the River Avon in Bath was designed by Robert Adam and built in 1769. It is built in the Palladian style and is one of the few remaining shop-lined bridges in the world. Bath is a prominent city on the tourist trail with its Roman Baths, Abbey and the Royal Crescent. The Kennet and Avon Canal passes through Sydney Gardens before losing its canal status at the River Avon at the foot of Bath Locks. Cleveland House (see left) in Sydney Gardens was once the headquarters of the Kennet and Avon Canal Company.

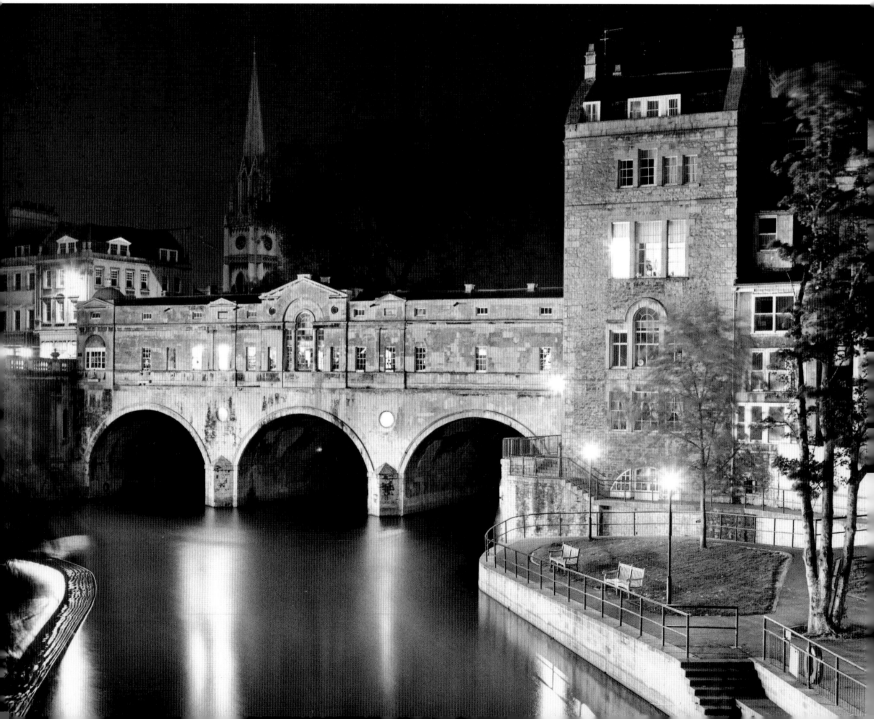

Mooring outside the George Inn at Bathampton on the Kennet and Avon Canal. The ten mile section between Bradford-on-Avon and Bath contains two major aqueducts over the Avon valley and some of the most dramatic scenery found anywhere on the British canals. The nearby pumping station at Claverton was built in 1810 and could pump 100,000 gallons of water from the River Avon into the canal, 47 feet above the river. A giant waterwheel that provided the power has been restored but the task has now been taken over by electrically controlled pumps.

Caen Hill Locks at Devizes on the Kennet and Avon Canal provide the best example to canal restorers that nothing is impossible. This formidable flight of locks was once totally derelict but is now back to full navigation. The Kennet and Avon was reopened in 1990 and connects the Thames at Reading to the Avon at Bath. It is 93 miles long and has 104 locks.

This lovely place on the River Wey is about as far south as you can travel by boat on the connected inland waterway system. The River Wey was one of the earliest river navigations in Britain. It opened from the Thames at Weybridge and ran to Guildford in 1653. It was extended to Godalming as the Godalming Navigation 80 years later. The waterway was privately owned for many years until 1964 when it was presented to the National Trust. Guildford is the only built-up part of the 20-mile navigation which mostly passes through beautiful Surrey countryside. It has junctions with the Basingstoke Canal and the disused Wey and Arun Canal.

Aylesford is on the tidal section of the River Medway. This beautiful river is one of the far flung outposts on the inland waterway system as it requires a potentially hazardous journey around the Thames estuary to reach it. Once into this delightful river there are over 40 miles of cruising waterway through the Garden of England. Tradition states that the river separates The Men of Kent from the Kentish Men. The Men of Kent are born on the eastern side of the river while the Kentish Men come from the west. The division originates when the Jutes partitioned Kent into two areas over 1,500 years ago. In 1066 it is said that the Men of Kent resisted the invading William the Conqueror with more verve than the Kentish Men who surrendered.

Walkers by the Basingstoke Canal near Winchfield. Towpath walking is generally on flat ground and so is very popular with people who are not into hill trekking. The seven miles between Crookham Wharf and Odiham Castle offers one of the finest stretches for boating or towpath walking in the country. The Basingstoke Canal reopened in 1991 following a massive rebuilding campaign by volunteers and two county councils. It is probably one of the most wooded canals, which is surprising as the first part between the River Wey and Fleet passes through a densely populated region.

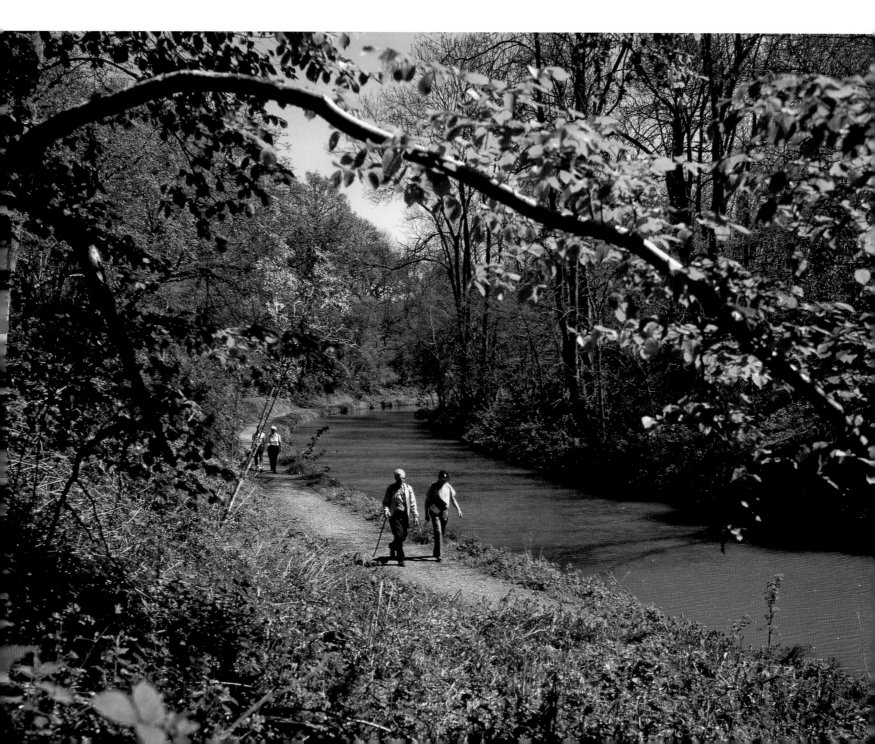

King Coal

A train of 'Tom Puddings' A train of 'Tom Puddings'
approaching Pollington Lock on the Aire and Calder Navigation in
1968. These floating containers were first invented around
1860 and each one was capable of carrying 40 tons of coal.
In 1913 there were over a thousand 'Tom Puddings' working
on the Yorkshire waterways. They were discontinued in 1986.
An example can be seen as an exhibit at the Yorkshire Waterway
Museum at Goole Docks.

Coal was the most important commodity carried on Britain's inland waterways. Over the years the Yorkshire waterways have carried vast quantities of coal to fuel Britain's industry and also for export. The black and white photo (right) shows a coal compartment on the Aire and Calder Navigation at Castleford in July 1968 when coal was still the most important cargo carried on the waterway. The colour photo (below) that was taken from the same position in 2003 shows a loaded sand and gravel barge. The navigation is still a commercial waterway but most of the collieries have closed down and coal carrying is now just a memory.

A busy scene at Ferrybridge 'C' power station on the Aire and Calder Navigation in July 1982. Coal barges wait to be unloaded at the wharf while an empty coal barge passes an oil tanker. The power station no longer operates on fossil fuel so coal is not required any more. Most of the former loading wharves have since been planted with trees and landscaped. In November 1965 three cooling towers collapsed in a high wind and were completely destroyed.

The Goole Boat Hoist emptying coal from 'Tom Puddings' into a collier ship in May 1974. 'Tom Puddings' were taken to Goole Docks and then each container was lifted from the water and tipped into the ship's hold. This was the last of five working hoists in Goole Docks and it has been preserved as an exhibit for the Yorkshire Waterway Museum. The museum tells the story of the Port of Goole, the transportation of coal and the lives of barge and boating families. The town and port owes its very existence to the arrival of the Aire and Calder Navigation in 1826. Before then Goole was a mere village nestling in the marshes beside the River Ouse.

Cut and Fill

The Shropshire Union Canal at Gnosall in August 1978. Some housing developments have occurred beyond the bridge but apart from several towpath improvements and an extension to the pub's garden, little has changed here in over 25 years. Gnosall, with its waterside pubs, is a favourite stopping place for visiting boaters. It has a 15th century church with a nearby lock-up building. Shelmore Embankment about a mile and a ha[lf] north of Gnosall was one of the major achievements in building the canal. Constant collapsing of the deep cutting meant that Shelmore was the last obstacle in completing the waterway which eventually opened in 1835.

The Birmingham and Liverpool Junction Canal was one of the last canals to be built in Britain. Engineered by Thomas Telford and completed in 1835, it ignored the contoured ramblings of its predecessors by hardly deviating from a straight line. Telford's 'cut and fill' technique built deep cuttings and high embankments. When locks were needed they were built in flights. The Birmingham and Liverpool connected the Staffs and Worcester Canal at Wolverhampton to the old Chester Canal at Nantwich. The Chester Canal was built much earlier between Nantwich and Ellesmere Port. In later years the two canals combined as the Shropshire Union Canal.

Cowley Cutting on the Shropshire Union Canal ends with a tunnel before entering Gnosall village. This is one of several deep cuttings on this canal. Although canal building techniques were much improved since Brindley's day, digging precipitous gorges like this was still done by pick, shovel and wheelbarrows.

The Boat Museum at Ellesmere Port is where the Shropshire Union Canal meets the Manchester Ship Canal. It spreads over seven acres of this former transhipment port. It has the world's largest floating collection of canal craft with eight indoor exhibitions inside historic buildings. The museum also has a working forge, craft workshops and a row of cottages representing different decades of the Victorian era.

Right: The Shropshire Union Canal at Tyrley Locks near Market Drayton. Five locks drop the canal through a beautiful sandstone cutting. The cavernous Woodseaves Cutting can be found just south of Tyrley Top Lock. Market Drayton was the birthplace of Robert Clive who became known as Clive of India (1725–1774). As a young man in the 1850s he fought the French in India, eventually clearing the way for British rule for the next hundred years. Market Drayton is also renowned for it cheese and gingerbread.

The Boat Horse

Before the advent of powered boats, it was horse-power that moved the canal boats. The horse became one of the family and it was often the job of the boatman's children to lead the horse along the towpath. Many tunnels had no towpath so the horse had to be led over the top while the boatman 'legged' his craft underground.

Boat horses required stabling at night and stables were provided at wharves and canalside pubs. Blacksmiths were needed to replace worn out shoes and corn needed to be available to feed the horses. Many of the older generation of boatmen didn't like what they called 'them new-fangled motors' and carried on working with horses well into the 20th century.

Below: The last working boat horse on the Black Country Canals at Smethwick Locks in December 1970. This boat carried rubbish on the Birmingham Canal. Experienced horses working along a familiar route would remember where to stop or slow down without anyone having to lead them. A working horse like this one would know when to stop at the approach to a lock.

Left: A legacy of the days of horse boating can be seen in many places on the canals with grooving on bridge plates like this one on the Shropshire Union Canal. Constant rubbing by taut wet towropes has eaten into the cast iron plate put there to protect the brick or stonework of the bridge.

Below: 'Bonnie' the boat horse pulling boat *Maria* near Ivinghoe on the Grand Union Canal. They were travelling from Manchester to London for a boat rally in July 2000.

Horse-drawn boat _Hyades_ on the Grand Union Canal at Fenny Stratford, Bletchley in June 1973. Young enthusiasts were trying to revive the art of commercial trading using a boat horse in the traditional manner. In general boat horses were hard worked but well looked after. There were exceptions as noted by Arnold Bennett in July 1873 – almost exactly a hundred years earlier than this photograph. He described a scene on the Trent and Mersey Canal in the Potteries where 'an unhappy skeleton of a horse floundered in a towpath quagmire being whipped by a seven-year old girl around its crooked large jointed legs'.

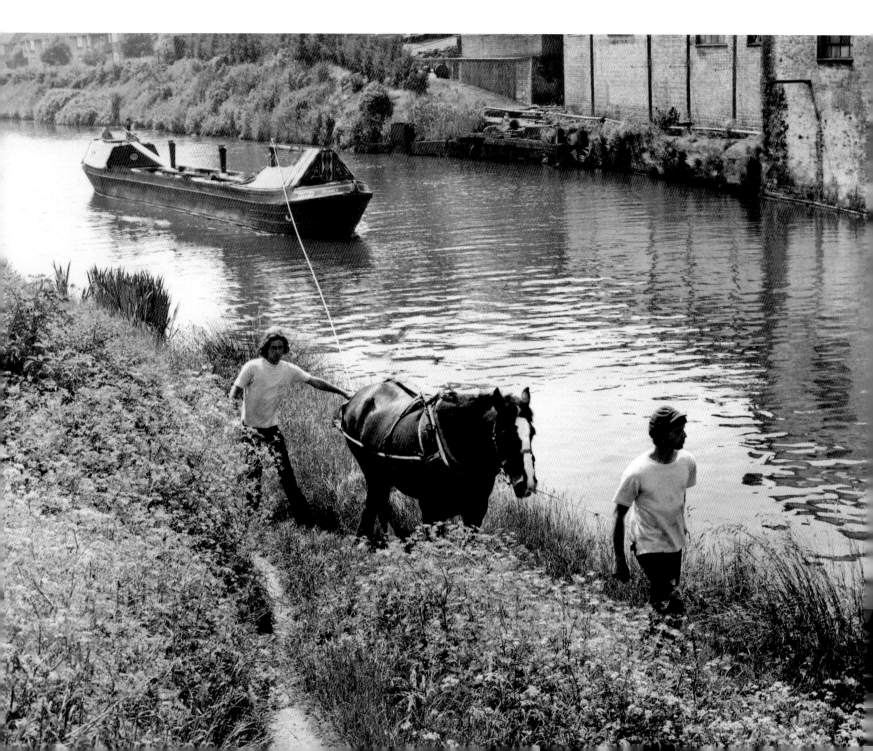

Left: The Kennet Valley horse-drawn trip boat operates from Kintbury on the Kennet and Avon Canal. It is available for hire between April and October and can accommodate 70 passengers.

Below: **Horse-drawn boats** can still be seen at various places on the inland waterways pulling public trip boats. This one was on the Ashby Canal near the Bosworth Battlefield site. Unfortunately the service has been discontinued.

Steam Boats

With steam belching out from every orifice, the splendid steam dredger *Perseverance* is seen here working on the Basingstoke Canal in October 1980. This 70 ton pontoon dredger worked for 15 years digging out sludge and silt from the western part of the Basingstoke Canal. The Canal was eventually reopened in 1991. The dredger is now an exhibit in the Boat Museum at Ellesmere Port.

Above: After twenty years rotting away in a Thames backwater, steam driven narrowboat *Tixall* has been restored and was seen here at Napton on the Oxford Canal on its way to a new home in August 2005.

Steam Puffer VIC 32 leaving Laggan Locks on the Caledonian Canal in the Scottish Highlands. The VIC series of Clyde Puffers was built to service warships during World War II. VIC is an acronym for Victualler Inshore Craft. Built in 1939, *VIC 32* carried ammunition and fuel during the war. Since 1975 it has been used as a pleasure boat taking steam enthusiasts on cruises around the Western Isles and the Crinan and Caledonian Canals.

Steam driven narrowboat *President* at Wolverhampton Locks. *President* was built in 1909 by the famous canal carrying company Fellows Morton and Clayton, who built 31 similar craft between 1889 and 1931. Although they were very powerful, steam narrowboats could only carry 12 tons compared with 25 by a horse-drawn boat. The boat is now owned by the Black Country Museum.

Restoration

The Wey and Arun Navigation is currently one of the most active restoration schemes. When it is eventually completed, it will reunite the River Wey and the rest of the inland waterway system with the south coast at Littlehampton. A section of canal at Loxwood has been restored with new locks and an aqueduct.

Drungewick Aqueduct under construction in 2002. The aqueduct has since been completed. It is used by the Wey and Arun Canal Trust Boat for passenger trips on the restored section at Loxwood.

elow: Rebuilt Flood Gate
idge at Orfold - Wey and
un Navigation in 2003.

Left: Graham Palmer, complete with trademark woolly hat, at the Stratford-upon-Avon Canal in April 1976. Graham was the founder and inspiration of the Waterway Recovery Group. Sometimes called 'The Dirty Weekenders', these hard working volunteers have been at the heart of every successful restoration project since 1970. The store hut and WC is named Melbury House, which was an irreverent joke aimed at the headquarters of the British Waterways Board. Graham Palmer died in 1988 at the early age of 48.

Above: A new lock on the northern section of the Montgomery Canal was named Graham Palmer Lock. There is a plaque to the memory of the founder of the Waterway Recovery Group – complete with woolly hat!

Right: Waterway Recovery Group volunteers working at Wilmcote Locks on the Stratford-upon-Avon Canal in 1976.

ne of the major
estoration stories in recent
ears was the successful
turn to navigation of the
ennet and Avon Canal.
ight: Widmead Lock
ear Newbury was one
f the last locks to be
ompleted. This picture
hows work in progress at
idmead Lock in
arch 1990.

Below: Digging a new channel at Moira at the top of the Ashby
Canal in July 2001. The present lock-free Ashby Canal ends at
Snarestone but an isolated section at Moira has been restored.
It was necessary to construct a new lock in order to continue the
canal northwards. A new section of canal will have to be built around
the town of Measham before the two separate parts of the Ashby
Canal can be completed.

This plaque at Tardebigge Top Lock on the Worcester and Birmingham Canal commemorates the famous meeting in 1946 between Robert Aickman and Tom and Angela Rolt that led to the founding of the Inland Waterways Association.

LTC Rolt wrote a book *Narrow Boat* about his travels around the decaying canal system in 1939 on board his boat *Cressy*. This plaque at Tom Rolt Bridge in Banbury is but a few yards from Tooley's Boatyard where his voyage began. Tom Rolt, Robert Aickman and waterway historian Charles Hadfield formed the Inland Waterways Association in 1946. The IWA campaigned to increase the national awareness of canals and their future in leisure and commerce. Without their efforts, officialdom would have allowed most of the remaining canals to run down towards final abandonment.

Right: Volunteers restoring a lock at Hanbury on the Droitwich Canal. When restored the Droitwich Canals will provide a picturesque short cut between the Worcester and Birmingham Canal and the River Severn.

Painted Boats

A working narrowboat was 70 feet long and 7 feet wide. The boatman's cabin was 8 to 9 feet long and less than 7 feet wide, and this tiny cabin was home to the boatman and his family. It was a life of hard work, low pay and dirty cargoes like coal, so it is not surprising that the boat people felt the need to brighten their lives by painting their home in bright colours. They painted bold designs in contrasting colours and developed the traditional 'Roses and Castle' theme which is an art form exclusive to canal boats.

Wooden tank narrow-boat *Gifford* at Braunston on the Grand Union Canal. These unpowered butty boats were built by Thomas Clayton to carry bulk liquids like tar and crude oil. *Gifford* is now owned by the Boat Museum Society.

A waterway artist painting a water can outside the Canal Museum at Stoke Bruerne on the Grand Union Canal.
A boatman often painted his name on the water can so it was easily identified in case of theft from its place on the cabin roof. A water can had several domestic uses, from peeling potatoes to washing the boatman's socks. A second can was used purely for drinking water.

Above: A fanciful scene on a boat cabin depicting a mediaeval castle with a canal bridge in the foreground.

Right: A colourful privately owned boat on the Trent and Mersey Canal. Note the painted tiller, the cabin doors, and a glimpse of brasswork in the cabin's interior.

Below: A pair of hotel boats at Braunston on the Grand Union Canal. Hotel boats are usually very colourful and well presented by their owners. Hotel boating is an ideal holiday for people who don't want the trouble of handling a boat or working locks. You can enjoy a holiday just looking at the passing scenery, reading a book and waiting to be fed.

The Anderton Lift

The Anderton Boat Lift near Northwich in Cheshire was built in 1865 to connect the Trent and Mersey Canal to the River Weaver 50 feet below. The Lift was modernised in 1908 and remained until corrosion forced its closure in 1983. It was restored in 2002 at a cost of £10 million with the 1908 structure and gears retained as a static monument.

Left: A section of the iron gearing on top of the Anderton Lift.

Below: The Anderton Lift and adjacent depot with a coaster in May 1968. The depot is now a freight terminal for road vehicles and the wharf is only used for storage.

A boat prepares to enter the restored Anderton Lift in June 2005. A trip boat takes visitors for a cruise down the river followed by a ride on the Lift. A new exhibition centre explains the history of the Lift, which has now become one of the main tourist attractions in this part of Cheshire.

Aqueducts

Below: A pair of narrowboats cross the North Circular Aqueduct in London in August 1980. This aqueduct was built in 1933 when the North Circular Road was constructed. It was replaced by a bigger one 60 years later when the road was widened. Removing the old aqueduct and getting the new one into place without interrupting traffic on one of London's busiest roads, proved to be a masterpiece of ingenuity.

Left: The new North Circular Aqueduct is considerably wide than the original and has two channels for the boats. It is the onl large structure on the lock-free Paddington Canal that runs from Bulls Bridge, Southall, to Little Venice.

Marple Aqueduct on the Lower Peak Forest Canal near Stockport. It was built in 1800 and took seven years to complete. Seven men were killed during its construction. The aqueduct spans the deep, wooded gorge of the River Goyt, and the holes in the stone abutments are to relieve pressure on the arches. This picture was taken in May 1974 shortly after the canal had been reopened following years of neglect. The Lower Peak Forest Canal is now part of the popular Cheshire Ring cruising circuit.

The English author George Borrow saw Marple Aqueduct and wrote *'Few things so beautiful in their origins as this canal, which it be known, with its locks and aqueducts, the grandest of which is the stupendous erection near Stockport'*.

Above and right: Pontcysyllte is the longest, highest and most famous of Britain's aqueducts. 1007 feet in length and 126 feet high, it carries the Llangollen Canal across the Valley of the River Dee. It was designed by Thomas Telford and William Jessop and was completed in 1805. Boats travel in a cast iron trough which has a suspended towpath on one side but nothing but space on the other. It leaves the boat's helmsman with a vertigo-inducing view of the valley below.

The engineer John Rennie built several aqueducts on the Lancaster and Kennet and Avon Canals. Dundas aqueduct near Bath on the Kennet and Avon is one of his finest. It was built in golden Bath stone which proved to be unsuitable for long lasting wear. Rennie wanted to build in brick but the canal company overruled him. It was opened in 1800 but required treatment for frost damage within three years. Despite structural patching over the years, Dundas Aqueduct, with its balustrades and cornices, remains one of Rennie's masterpieces. It was named after Charles Dundas who was the original chairman of the Kennet and Avon Canal Company and in 1951 became the first canal structure to be scheduled as an ancient monument.

Waterside Inns

The Angel on the Bridge by the River Thames at Henley. There are more famous and historic inns on the river but few have a more advantageous position than the Angel. You will need to get here early for a seat on the terrace during the Henley Regatta in July. The Henley Regatta began in 1839 and received Royal patronage by Prince Albert in 1851. Henley staged the Olympic rowing events at the 1908 and 1948 London Games. The 2012 Olympic rowing events will take place at the new Eton/Dorney course.

Above: The Union Inn at Aylestone, Leicester, shows a working boat being gauged to assess the amount of tonnage it is carrying.

Above: The Eight Locks pub at Ryders Green in the heart of the Black Country.

The Globe Inn at Linslade on the Grand Union Canal started as a beerhouse for the navvies when the canal was being dug. It was called the Globe Beer Shop in 1841 and in later years provided stables for the boatmen's horses. The stables were converted to an extra bar in 1969. It has an attractive setting next to the canal as it passes through the wooded River Ouzel valley. The pub has become very popular in recent years and is festooned with flowers during the summer months.

Left: The Boat Inn
at Berkhamsted on the
Grand Union Canal.

In his book *Narrow Boat*, LTC Rolt describes the Cross Keys
at Penkridge on the Staffs and Worcester Canal. This was during
his epic voyage around the decaying canals in 1939. He
described the pub as 'a little canal inn standing amid the fields
beside the towpath waiting for boats that never came'. Mr Rolt
would still have recognised the pub when this picture was taken
in August 1978. Since then, the pub has considerably enlarged
and has been engulfed by a housing estate. It is now a popular
stopping place for visiting boaters.

Right: The derelict Barge Inn, at Seend Cleeve by the equally derelict Kennet and Avon Canal in March 1973. The pub was reopened in time for the restoration of the canal in 1990. Fred Kempster, who was 8 feet 5 inches tall and Britain's tallest man, once lived at the Barge Inn around the time of the First World War.

Below: The Barge Inn at Seend Cleeve in 1990. This very busy scene was taken shortly after the canal was reopened. It was a time when everyone who had a boat wanted to cruise the Kennet and Avon Canal. This beautiful navigation has now established itself as one of the most popular cruising waterways.

Waterways in Winter

Boats ploughing through the ice in December 1981 at Denham on the Grand Union Canal. Conditions like these were a nightmare for the working boatman who had to cope with iced up canals and frozen locks. Self-employed boatmen were only paid on delivery of cargo, so being frozen up meant loss of income. The severe winter of 1963 ended regular commercial trading on the narrow canals.

Right: Somerton Deep Lock on the Oxford Canal. This section of the Oxford Canal is very open and exposed to wintry weather. It is likely that an ice-breaker would have worked on sections like these in the days of commercial trading in an effort to keep the canal open.

A frozen Tring Summit on the Grand Union Canal. This canal was the main water highway between the Midland coal fields and the south. Delays in delivery because of freezing conditions meant customers would look elsewhere for supplies and so the canals lost trade to the more reliable railways.

Right: Little Bedwyn on the Kennet and Avon Canal. This pa of the canal is especially busy on Good Friday when the Devize to Westminster canoe race passes here. On a bleak late afternoon in January, only dog walkers and the odd waterway photographer ventures out on to the towpath.

A cormorant poses in front of Canary Wharf by the River Thames. Cormorants, once a winter visitor to the inland waterways, have become common throughout the year, especially on the River Thames.

Waterway Flora and Fauna

Left: A heron patiently waits for his dinner by the Grand Union Canal at Tring. The grey heron is one of Britain's largest waterside birds and is very common beside the rivers and canals of England and Wales. It prefers to hunt alone, standing motionless in shallow water, waiting for unwary fish to appear near the surface.

Below: A swan admires its reflection in the River Thames. The annual ceremony of swan upping takes place on the Thames for six days on the first week in July. The purpose of swan upping is to mark all new cygnets with the same mark as their parents to ascertain ownership. On the Thames, the Queen shares ownership of mute swans with the Vintners' and Dyers' companies. The shared right of ownership was granted in the 15th century.

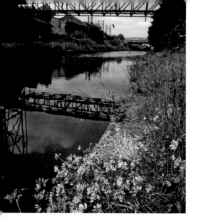

Left: Bird's-foot-trefoil is commonly called the 'egg and bacon' plant, because of its colours. It is a member of the pea family and is very common in coastal regions. The flowers in the picture are growing by the industrial Tame Valley Canal in the Black Country, a long way from the coast. A surprising variety of wild flowering plants can be found on the banks of Black Country canals.

Below: This flourishing scene is not what one would expect to see by the Aire and Calder Navigation in such a dour place as Knottingley. Local people with permission from British Waterways have planted the towpath with flowers. The result is a startling floral display that would have been acceptable at any national flower show.

Into the 21st Century

Many big city canals went into decline during the mid 20th century and became rubbish-filled ditches. In many cases the public were denied access to the towpaths. Now, in the 21st century, people are actively encouraged to visit the canals.

This has led to the construction of spectacular tubular steel footbridges like these at Castlefield, Manchester and Apsley on the Grand Union Canal.

The Glaxo Building
at the Great West Road,
Brentford, has a long
frontage by the Grand Union
Canal. Modern office buildings built on old factory
sites are appearing all over
the canal system. Instead
of wharves for transporting
goods they landscape their
waterside for the benefit
of their workers and to
enhance the appearance
of the company.

Left: In its commercial heyday, Paddington Basin was one of the busiest places on the canals. A warehouse-flanked pool was crammed with boats loading and unloading coal, sand, timber and bricks. There would have been horses everywhere pulling boats, carts or waiting to be stabled. With the decline of waterborne trade the basin fell into sharp decline and was closed off from the public gaze. Now renamed Paddington Waterside it has become one of Europe's biggest urban regeneration schemes. When completed there will be offices, shops, restaurants, bars and hotels. It has already been reopened to the public who can use some of the innovative bridges that have been constructed. The unique helix bridge which rotates and retracts on a steel corkscrew can be seen in the middle of the photograph.

Below: The Oracle Centre by the Kennet and Avon Canal in Reading. Shopping areas like this are built around a waterway with waterside seating and cafes. Similar examples can be found at Banbury on the Oxford Canal and Merry Hill on the Dudley Canal in the West Midlands.

Left: The Lancaster Canal was an isolated waterway cut off from the rest of the system until the building of the Ribble Link in 2002. A small stream called the Savick Brook was canalised and made navigable by constructing a number of locks. This raised the new waterway from the River Ribble to the Lancaster Canal on the outskirts of Preston. Boats can now reach the Lancaster Canal via the Leeds and Liverpool Canal, the River Douglas and the River Ribble. The success of the Ribble Link has given hope to proposed new canals such as the Bedford and Grand Union Link to Milton Keynes which would provide an alternative route into the Fenland waterways.

Below: The restoration of the Huddersfield Narrow Canal required a new section of canal through the centre of Slaithwaite. There are several superb mills in the vicinity of the canal and a floating tearoom where visitors can sit and watch the world go by. The town is often used as a location for film companies, and it was once the home of Bamforths who were famous for their saucy seaside postcards.

The Falkirk Wheel is the world's first rotating boat lift and a masterpiece of modern engineering. Two counterbalanced water-filled caissons rotate within the wheel which uses gravity to keep the boats level. Only a tiny amount of electricity is required to get the operation started. The Falkirk Wheel provides the link between two restored canals reconnecting Glasgow and Edinburgh by water after years of dereliction. Opened in 2002, it has already become the second biggest tourist attraction in Scotland after Edinburgh Castle.

The Falkirk Wheel aqueduct carries boats from the top of the wheel a tunnel underneath both the Antonine Wall and railway. Then there are two locks raising boats to the Union Canal level. After that there are 32 lock-free miles all the way into Edinburgh.

Index